T0318228

Negotiating the Environment

Civil society participants have voiced concerns that the environmental problems that were the subject of multilateral environmental agreements negotiated during the 1992 Rio processes are not serving to ameliorate global environmental problems. These concerns raise significant questions regarding the utility of negotiating agreements through the UN. This book elucidates the complexity of how participants engage in these negotiations through the various processes that take place under the auspices of the UN—primarily those related to climate and biological diversity.

By taking an ethnographic approach and providing concrete examples of how it is that civil society participants engage in making policy, this book develops a robust sense of the implications of the current terrain of policy-making—both for the environment, and for the continued participation of non-state actors in multilateral environmental governance. Using data gathered at actual negotiations, the book develops concepts such as participation and governance beyond theory. The research uses participant observation ethnographic methods to tie the theoretical frameworks to people's actual activities as policy is generated and contested.

Whereas topics associated with global environmental governance are traditionally addressed in fields such as international relations and political science, this book contributes to developing a richer understanding of the theories using a sociological framework, tying individual activities into larger social relations and shedding light on critical questions associated with transnational civil society and global politics.

Lauren E. Eastwood is Associate Professor in the Department of Sociology at the State University of New York at Plattsburgh, USA.

Routledge Focus on Environment and Sustainability

For more information about this series, please visit:
https://www.routledge.com/Routledge-Focus-on-Environment-and-Sustainability/book-series/RFES

Negotiating the Environment

Civil Society, Globalisation
and the UN

Lauren E. Eastwood

Routledge
Taylor & Francis Group

LONDON AND NEW YORK

First published 2019
by Routledge

2 Park Square, Milton Park, Abingdon, Oxfordshire OX14 4RN
52 Vanderbilt Avenue, New York, NY 10017

Routledge is an imprint of the Taylor & Francis Group, an informa business

First issued in paperback 2020

Copyright © 2019 Lauren E. Eastwood

British Library Cataloguing-in-Publication Data
A catalogue record for this book is available from the British Library

Library of Congress Cataloging-in-Publication Data
A catalog record has been requested for this book

ISBN: 978-0-415-66056-3 (hbk)
ISBN: 978-0-367-60660-2 (pbk)

Typeset in Times New Roman
by Out of House Publishing

This book is dedicated to activists who are working to make the world a better place, whether within the halls of UN negotiations, or 'on the ground' in specific locations: your work is so important.

Contents

Acknowledgements

Anyone who has written a sole-authored book knows that, in so many ways, that phrase 'sole-authored' is deceiving. It would be hard to prioritise the types of necessary support—from the more tangible aspects such as funding and editing, to the equally crucial emotional ones.

I must acknowledge my friends—in particular those with whom I run, bike, and swim—as I leaned on this training as a therapeutic crutch. Erin Campbell and Linda Shepard—you both always had faith in me—on the road and behind the computer. Friend and colleague support from Autumn Bennet, Margaret Hanshaw, Doreen Martinez, Leanne Macey, Elizabeth Onasch, Diane Fine, and Ryan Alexander has also been much appreciated, particularly when I saw the light at the end of the tunnel yet constantly feared the train would become derailed.

My appreciation also extends to my dear friend Rebecca Wolff, who read several of the first drafts of chapters and gave helpful suggestions. Through this process, as with my dissertation years ago, I have valued immensely the continued support of my former graduate school adviser and current friend, Marj DeVault. Nancy Naples has also assuaged my panic and supported my work in ways that have truly helped me get back into the project when I've lost sight of my main objectives and gotten discouraged.

Former students James Richmond and Steffaney Wilcox also helped with some of the aspects of the manuscript, as did Kimberly Bailey, who wrangled my citations and bibliographies into Harvard format.

My most heartfelt and sincere thanks go to my parents: Lynn and Greg Eastwood. In terms of the types of support I listed at the start of these acknowledgements, they have provided all of the above. Most importantly, they have always expressed their love for me and their faith in me. Every day I appreciate the support of my family—including that of my sisters—Kristen and Kara. They are people I can lean on, and I have done substantial leaning throughout this book project.

In terms of financial support, from 2009 to 2011, the data I gathered was assisted by a grant from the Abe Fellowship Program administered by the Social Science Research Council and the American Council of Learned Societies in cooperation with and with funds provided by the Japan Foundation Center for Global Partnership.

I would like to express appreciation for the Griffith Climate Response Fellowship that I received in the autumn of 2014, as the research I conducted with Dr Timothy Cadman through Griffith University in Brisbane, Australia, was extremely helpful. Funding, as a part of this fellowship, to attend the COP20 (Twentieth Conference of Parties) UN Climate Meetings in Lima, Peru, was invaluable as well. Tim Cadman deserves thanks not only as a fellow researcher but as an almost-brother, whose friendship I value immeasurably. Some financial support was also obtained through State University of New York (SUNY) College at Plattsburgh in the form of small grants and Redcay Faculty/Student Research Fellowships.

I want also to acknowledge the assistance of several organisations that were kind enough to provide me with the needed credentials in order to access the UN meetings. First and foremost, I must highlight the support of Marilyn Averill, who not only facilitated my access to several UN-based climate negotiations (through the University of Colorado, Boulder) but also served as a wealth of knowledge about the current state of all things UNFCCC (United Nations Framework Convention on Climate Change). Also providing access to the climate negotiations were GlobalWarmingSolution.org, Community Forestry International, The Institute of Cultural Affairs, Ghana, Women Organizing for Change in Agriculture and Natural Resource Management, and EcoArts. Access to Convention on Biological Diversity (CBD) meetings was obtained through the Center for Earth and Environmental Science at SUNY College at Plattsburgh. Access to the UN Forum on Forests and the UN Permanent Forum on Indigenous Issues was provided by the Association of Third World Studies (now the Association of Global South Studies). Lastly, portions of Chapter 3 previously appeared in Eastwood, L.E. (2011) 'Climate Change Negotiations and Civil Society Participation: Shifting and Contested Terrain', *Theory in Action: Journal of the Transformative Studies Institute*, 4 (1): 8–42.

Figures

Abbreviations

ABS	Access and Benefit-Sharing
AGCI	Amsterdam Global Change Institute
AHEG	Ad Hoc Expert Group
AOSIS	Alliance Of Small Island States
AWG	Ad-Hoc Working Group
CAN	Climate Action Network
CBD	Convention on Biological Diversity
COP	Conference of Parties
CRP	conference-room paper
CSD	Commission on Sustainable Development
CSO	civil society organisations
ECOSOC	Economic and Social Council (to the General Assembly of the United Nations)
EU	European Union
G77	Group of 77
GMO	genetically modified organisms
ICAO	International Civil Aviation Organization
IFC	International Facilitating Committee
IFF	Intergovernmental Forum on Forests
ILC	indigenous and local communities
IMF	International Monetary Fund
IPBES	Intergovernmental Platform on Biodiversity and Ecosystem Services
IPCC	Intergovernmental Panel on Climate Change
IPF	Intergovernmental Panel on Forests
IPLC	indigenous peoples and local communities
IPO	Indigenous Peoples' organisation
LCA	long-term cooperative action
MEA	Multilateral Environmental Agreement
MGI	Major Group Initiative

NGO	non-governmental organisation
REDD	Reduced Emissions from Deforestation and forest Degradation
RINGOS	Research and Independent Non-Governmental Organisations
SBI	Subsidiary Body for Implementation
SBSTA	Subsidiary Body for Scientific and Technological Advice
SBSTTA	Subsidiary Body on Scientific, Technical, and Technological Advice
SDG	Sustainable Development Goals
SIDS	Small Island Developing States
UNCED	United Nations Conference on Environment and Development
UNDRIP	United Nations Declaration on the Rights of Indigenous Peoples
UNEP	United Nations Environment Program
UNFCCC	United Nations Framework Convention on Climate Change
UNFF	United Nations Forum on Forests
UNPFII	United Nations Permanent Forum on Indigenous Issues
WEF	World Economic Forum
WIPO	World Intellectual Property Organization
WRI	World Resources Institute
WRM	World Rainforest Movement
WTO	World Trade Organization
WWF	World Wildlife Fund

1 The politics of nature and the nature of politics

There is no question that the climate negotiations are dealing with a very important political reality. However, that reality pales in comparison to the reality presented by physics and chemistry. Frankly, I don't think that the natural world is going to budge on its negotiating position.

(Bill McKibben field notes, 29 November 2010)

What does it mean to 'make policy' through the UN? How do UN environmental negotiations actually work? What is at stake as delegates and credentialed participants make their way to a Conference of Parties ('COP' as delegates say) located in a city that likely requires extensive travel for the majority of the attendees? The world of policy-making is a strange and complex one. It is a world that is often simultaneously mundane and fascinating. This is a world that is marked by intensity and focus—as participants gather for intensive and focused discussions of texts, where rest is hard to come by, and constant strategic manoeuvring is expected and anticipated. This is a world where people's talk is punctuated with acronyms and jargon. In fact, the talk becomes so specialised that when one stops to think about it, one notes that discussions remain largely focused on language associated with particular agenda items. This language is abstracted from actual geographical locations and references to identifiable cases of environmental degradation. The uninformed observer would be lost and confused, wondering what the discussions had to do with climate, biological diversity, or forests, since policy talk brings participants into a specialised realm that seems strikingly disconnected from specific environmental problems.

What are the implications of what gets accomplished in this world for 'on-the-ground' realities? Regardless of whether the negotiations involve 'hard' or 'soft' law, there is no 'International Court of Environmental Justice' designed to arbitrate and litigate lack of adherence to any given Declaration, Convention, Agreement, or Accord. Yet negotiations continue, and delegates debate for hours whether the appropriate word in a given paragraph will be 'can' or 'may', 'should' or 'shall'. This is a world that is well known by few—but those who engage regularly in this arena have sophisticated, in-depth work knowledges of the intricacies of agenda items and alphabet-soup lexicons. Participants work hard to find the exact term that can say enough to gain an agreement among governments but yet not too much to cross other delegations' 'red lines', thus jeopardising the possibility of achieving the oft-elusive Consensus Agreement.

Clearly, international environmental deliberations are inherently messy, as governments' negotiating positions are based on a range of interests that become entangled in such dynamics as foreign relations, global economic downturns, fossil-fuel-based infrastructures, and historical development inequities, among myriad other intensely complex issues. This book is situated in the centre of this broad and convoluted context, where debates about the environment have profound significance on a political level, as nation-states come to the table with particular agendas and mandates. The implications of these intergovernmental negotiations on the ground—at the local level in specific locations—are less obvious and more difficult to track. Yet it is clear that, regardless of the relative obscurity of these deliberations and the regular intransigence of governments to make environmental commitments that are consistent with environmental science, the majority of the participants are largely unwilling to fully abandon the UN as an intergovernmental realm providing a space for potential social or environmental change.

This book speaks to the complexity of these issues by taking an explicitly ethnographic approach to researching, analysing, and writing about UN environmental policy. Based on data collected within the halls and meeting rooms of UN negotiations that have been held in various locations around the world, the analysis presented here is intended to contribute to broader discussions of global environmental governance, in part by bringing readers into the processes themselves. The ontology of ethnography oriented my data collection as I attended meetings associated with the United Nations Framework Convention on Climate Change (UNFCCC), UN Convention on Biological Diversity (CBD), United Nations Forum on Forests (UNFF), and the United Nations Permanent Forum on Indigenous Issues (UNPFII).[1] I utilise these data to engage in conversations about such dynamics as civil society participation in global environmental governance, the relevance and role of science in policy processes, and the meaning of multilateral negotiations in a world impacted by the economic trends of neoliberal globalisation. Interspersed in my analysis are what I call 'ethnographic snippets', which are largely in the present tense and are thus designed to bring the reader into the actual site of my research. In the spirit of ethnography, I use these rich descriptions of actual experiences to illustrate the settings where the type of work on which I focus in this manuscript gets done.

Throughout my research, I specifically kept an analytic eye on the work of those who have engaged in the process as UN-designated 'non-governmental' participants—members of civil society organisations (CSOs) and Indigenous Peoples' organisations (IPOs) whose engagement with policy negotiations was designed to strategically contribute to the environmental policy-making processes and influence policy outcomes yet who often brought a set of concerns to the table that were different than the concerns of many governments.

To some degree, as I have analysed the data, I have also drawn on prior participant observation research conducted in meetings associated with bodies such as the Commission on Sustainable Development (CSD) and the predecessor body to the UNFF, the Intergovernmental Forum on Forests (IFF), as these and other UN-related fora have provided spaces for members of CSOs and IPOs to highlight issues of specific importance to them—issues that also intersect with the policy work of the UNFCCC, CBD, UNFF, and UNPFII.

As I have been attending UN meetings related to environmental and Indigenous Peoples' policy since 1998, I have a somewhat longitudinal view of the transformations in various dynamics over the past two decades. Gathered from inside the negotiations as I observed UN meetings held in Costa Rica, Denmark, Thailand, Japan, Canada, Ghana, Kenya, Mexico, Germany, Qatar, Poland, Peru, the United States, and France, the data are used to illustrate *how* policy-making gets done in a very literal and concrete sense. These data are the basis for insights into how 'global environmental governance' actually works in practice. The ethnographic elements of the book are designed to bring readers into the policy processes as I engage in my evaluation and analysis of some of the broader implications of the dynamics surrounding the deliberations.

Ethnography: Into the belly of the beast

Typically, as I have made my way through the hallways of the UN headquarters in New York or Geneva, I've thought of myself as being 'in the belly of the beast'—knowing that all around me work is being done to accomplish the 'work' of the UN. The underground meeting rooms and passageways that lead to mail centres, UN document centres, or various other offices, connect the range of activities to each other. As I emerged from a washroom in New York, for example, preparing to head back into negotiations of the UNFF, I encountered a film crew clustered around none other than actor George Clooney, who had come to the UN to advocate for a policy response to the atrocities in South Sudan. I've gotten lost in those hallways—both in New York and Geneva—as I have attempted to attend a meeting of non-governmental organisations (NGOs) or locate a photocopier to duplicate documents. The badge that lists my credentials has allowed me access to some areas and not others, making the shortest route to a particular destination often impossible. Even after all these years, I still feel most comfortable staking out a seat in the NGO-designated area of a meeting room, settling in with my earpiece for translations and armed with the most current negotiating text so that I can follow the 'interventions' (official statements) of participants in the various processes.

'Ethnographic snippet': UNFCCC COP16

Now, however, I'm out of the confined space of UN headquarters, yet somehow my 'site' is still marked by the mammoth intergovernmental bureaucracy that is the UN. I'm in Cancun, Mexico, attending UNFCCC COP16. It is December, and the palm trees lit up by tiny white lights at night seem contradictory, as I have spent the majority of my life in geographical regions where Christmas decorations are accompanied by snow and coniferous trees rather than sun and tourists. I have arrived at the actual meeting location by bus; the Mexican government has arranged for several transport loops to the major hotels in the area. Cancun, known as a destination for all-inclusive resorts, is now overrun by an odd mix of the usual revellers and those of us who are here not for the beachside margaritas but for the work that lies ahead over the two weeks of climate negotiations. Rather than beachwear and sunblock, our suitcases have carried our typical meeting-appropriate garb, laptops, and business cards. We have been notified by conference organisers that, due to the climate in Mexico, 'business casual' attire is acceptable.

Having been dropped off by the designated bus for my hotel's loop, I have come through security at the UN 'Cancunmesse'. I know what to expect as I have been doing this for several days now here in Cancun, and, more importantly, this is not my first foray into UN deliberations.

After going through security, as I make my way down the newly constructed corrugated-metal hallway brightly lit by fluorescent lights and past a high-tech exhibit scrolling through statistics and graphs related to civil society participation in past COPs, I'm struck by the fact that the UN COPs for climate negotiations seem to create a new infrastructure wherever they are held. Like a mini-Olympics, nation-states express their interest in hosting a climate COP, negotiate with the UNFCCC Secretariat, and, upon approval, the planning of logistics and construction of necessary infrastructure begins.

Clearly, in this case the Mexican government has learned from the debacle that was Copenhagen a year earlier, as far as space is concerned. While the Danes had created the 'Bella Center' for the 2009 COP15— an impressive and massive tent-like facility that contained restaurants, meeting rooms, exhibit halls, postal services, cyclists with bins of apples for sale, solar prototypes, delegation offices, and a range of other amenities that have become standard for these particular annual UN meetings—multiple dynamics came together in Copenhagen to create a context where participant interest overwhelmed space capacity. A growing public concern about governmental (and intergovernmental) inaction on climate change, an increased sense of urgency in light of increasingly dire scientific findings, and the key relevance of the agenda items for the 2009 COP meetings combined to create a dynamic where well over 30,000 individuals legitimately registered to attend COP15, yet the organisers argued that the venue could safely hold only approximately 11,000.

Not only did the negotiations themselves fall apart in Copenhagen as a result of a range of factors, some of which will be addressed later in this book, but organisers of COP15 were forced to restrict access to the Bella Center, much to the chagrin of those members of civil society who subsequently gained access only on a rationed basis through 'secondary badges', with many left out of the negotiations—relegated to venues around the city where webcasts of the unfolding deliberations provided excluded participants with a space to remain apprised from afar. The political turmoil related to tensions that arose around the negotiations themselves worsened as access was denied to thousands of participants. Regardless of the fact that the majority of these participants would not have had the opportunity to engage directly in the negotiations whether they had been in the conference room or not, people's perceptions of being 'inside' the meeting venue rather than relegated to a satellite location signalled the fact that space and location have meaning for those involved in these negotiations. Watching the negotiations from the back of the room in the actual venue versus observing the negotiations unfolding on a large screen in a separate location seemed somehow categorically different to participants, as their engagement with the negotiations were perceived to be lacking in legitimacy if they couldn't get 'inside' the Bella Center to engage with COP15.

A year later, in Cancun at COP16, it is evident that the Mexican government has taken measures to avoid the space capacity issues that exacerbated frustrations about political process in Copenhagen. In fact, there are *two* venues for COP16—strategically geographically removed from one another. Official negotiations on agenda-item texts are held at the Moon Palace Hotel, a sprawling complex with lodging and meeting-space options. However, I'm here at the 'Cancunmesse', a series of freshly built warehouse-sized buildings—also with meeting rooms and food options—where 'side event' presentations and exhibits are scheduled to take place. The Cancunmesse serves as all participants' point of entry to the negotiations. All delegates and credentialed participants, except for those who represent the highest level of government, must first go through the security process here at Cancunmesse before boarding yet another bus to travel approximately 15 kilometres to the site of the negotiations. No official negotiations take place in the Cancunmesse, yet talk of negotiations is constant. And side events, depending on their content, can be packed with participants.

The side event I've arrived to attend is not slated to start for another ten minutes, yet the room is full to overflowing as I approach along the meeting room hallway inside building D. I squeeze through the crowd of people chatting near the door to enter the room and notice a few empty chairs—predictably in the middle of rows of otherwise occupied seats. Some people have elected to stand along the walls rather than become mired in the middle of a row of seated people. I identify a seat that looks available, awkwardly make my way to the centre of the row and settle in. We're here for a presentation called 'Science-Based Long-Term Targets: Why They're Needed, How They Can Be Achieved' hosted by two civil society-based organisations: 350.org and the Center for Biological Diversity.

In contrast to the highly specialised and often seemingly obscure negotiations of text that takes place at all COPs, the side events tend to put aside the language of diplomacy in favour of presentations of research findings or innovative programmes that may be of interest to participants. Thus, while both side events and negotiations are equally 'political' in that they take up issues that are relevant to the negotiations, side events tend to engage with the politicised elements of the deliberations more openly so, as they are not bound by the same rules and expectations of diplomacy as text negotiations are. Here at COP16, presentations by the Rainforest Alliance, the Greenbelt Movement, the Third World Network, the Secretariats of the various UN Conventions, and myriad other organisations fill the time slots of the early afternoon break between official negotiations and into the evenings. These are often bypassed by delegates who are eager to get on the bus heading to the Moon Palace location, yet many participants make a point of attending side events in order to learn more about the broader terrain that circumscribes the actual negotiations.

It is evident, not only by the attendance but also by the feel of the energy in the room, that there is great interest in this particular side event. Much of the allure is related to the fact that Bill McKibben, founder of 350.org, is slated to speak. 350.org, an activist CSO that emerged in response to the inaction of governments on climate policy at regional, domestic, and intergovernmental levels, explicitly tied itself to climate science through its name: James Hansen's now iconic research that indicated that 350 parts per million of carbon-dioxide concentration in the atmosphere represents a climate threshold (Hansen et al., 2008). Higher concentrations of carbon dioxide would lead to conditions unlike those we have seen in human history by precipitating global average temperature rise that would, ultimately, have catastrophic consequences for the biosphere. This side event was explicitly designed to allow participants to discuss growing concerns—supported by the scientific community—regarding a rapidly changing climate in a context where, at the intergovernmental level, progress is impeded by the procedural need for governments with myriad conflicting political interests to come to a consensus.

As the side event started and McKibben began to speak, it was evident that his sentiments were shared by many in the room. 'Look', said McKibben in his matter-of-fact yet amiable style. 'There is no question that the climate negotiations are dealing with a very important political reality. However, that reality pales in comparison to the reality presented by physics and chemistry. Frankly, I don't think that the natural world is going to budge on its negotiating position.'[2] This statement was met with smiles and even some laughter, yet the significance and gravity of McKibben's point was well understood. Subsequent to this experience at COP16, this very argument has been reiterated by McKibben himself—including immediately after COP21 in December 2015. As the world was heralding the Paris Agreement as being an important step towards solving the climate crisis, McKibben's contribution to *The Guardian* articulated his concerns about world leaders, the lack of action on climate, and his critique of the UN process: 'There's no more compromises or trade-offs that can be made. You're no longer negotiating with a bunch of other countries around a conference table. You're negotiating with physics, and physics holds all the good cards' (McKibben 2015).

Like oil and water: Fossil-fuel-based politics versus environmental sustainability

A central organising dimension of this book involves tensions such as the one that McKibben has reiterated multiple times. Throughout my forays into UN meetings, I have been keenly aware of the tensions between political positions taken by governments and the realities of environmental degradation, and how participants strategically negotiate these conflicting dynamics. Indeed, such incongruities are part and parcel of UN deliberations. The contradiction between science and policy articulated by McKibben was regularly present in arguments made by government delegates and non-governmental participants alike.

Encapsulated in a simple protest sign seen during the march that took place in conjunction with COP15 in 2009 stating 'blah blah blah', the perception that policy talk fails to address the gravity of environmental degradation is widespread. While massive resources are poured into policy-making processes that take place under the auspices of the UN, and while policy-makers have identified objectives that speak to the urgency of environmental degradation, policy processes are inherently 'political' in the sense that they are necessarily embroiled in a range of dynamics that, according to some analysts and participants, render them unable to adequately arrest global environmental degradation (see, for example, Gunter 2004; Gale 2013; and Humphreys 1996, 2006). There are, indeed, opportunities for science to be brought into policy deliberations. Yet these opportunities are never divorced from the politics of intergovernmental negotiations. Never is science allowed to simply 'speak for itself' or to determine policy outcomes, as 'policy' shares its etymological root with 'politics' for reasons that become blatantly apparent when one observes global environmental governance in the making.

Indeed, many participants who engage in UN-based environmental policy negotiations remark upon the disjuncture between the often obscure and convoluted policy positions and current scientific knowledge of environmental degradation. The 'physical reality' of which McKibben speaks has been made increasingly evident through successive iterations of the assessment reports produced by the scientific body associated with the UNFCCC—the Intergovernmental Panel on Climate Change (IPCC) (see, for example, IPCC 2014). In an effort to better tie UN negotiations related to biological diversity to scientific evidence, the CBD recently initiated its own scientific body—the IPBES (Intergovernmental Platform on Biodiversity and Ecosystem Services). As is stated on the IPBES website,

> Biodiversity ... provides the basis for ecosystems and the services they provide that underpin human well-being. However, biodiversity and ecosystem services are declining at an unprecedented rate, and in order to address this challenge, adequate local, national and international policies need to be adopted and implemented. To achieve this, decision makers need scientifically credible and independent information that takes into account the complex relationships between biodiversity, ecosystem services, and people.
>
> (IPBES n.d.)

Here the implication is that science can offer an antidote to the political points of blockage that prevent agreement and subsequent action. At multiple points during negotiations associated with both the UNFCCC and the CBD, participants raised the importance of science in informing the work of policy-makers. Both the CBD and UNFCCC have 'scientific and technical' bodies which are intended to allow for more robust discussions of dynamics pertaining to science than are possible at the highly politicised COPs. Likewise, participants other than McKibben have taken up a rhetorical position that is designed to cut through the politics of negotiations by pointing out that the laws of science are not up for negotiation.

However, as was pointed out to me during my research by a member of a prominent environmental NGO, the climate negotiations intersect with the political realities of fossil-fuel-based economies in ways that clearly create intense conflicts for governments. This is due to the fact that governments' interests in maintaining a fossil-fuel-based energy infrastructure intersect strongly with their economic interests. This, in turn, creates a context whereby participants who are critical of the fundamental basis of the origins of anthropogenic climate change—primarily fossil-fuel use, deforestation, and current agricultural practices—are inherently in a position of coming up against an intensely powerful impasse. In spite of the scientific evidence, and the reality presented by physics and chemistry, the existing economic order that is *deeply* integrated with fossil-fuel-based energy resources creates a profound contradiction that policy-makers are largely unable to resolve within the context of UN environmental negotiations. A central argument of this book is that while it is obvious that the laws of nature trump the laws of human social organisation, *the political structures that are a product of hegemonic human social organisation at this current juncture of neoliberal globalisation remain intransigent in the face of ever more conclusive scientific evidence that those very structures are producing devastating environmental degradation.* This book seeks to use actual examples of negotiations to unpack many of the tensions associated with UN deliberations yet argues that the tension between a global economic structure that requires economic growth and the environmental problems these bodies are designed to debate exist as the most fundamental tension of all. Activist CSOs and scientists see the 'physical reality' of environmental degradation as becoming increasingly clearer as a result of the fact that burning fossil fuels, engaging in massive industrial agriculture, and continuing to denude forests so that they can no longer act as carbon sinks contributes to a changing climate. Participants in negotiations surrounding biological diversity can point to ever more dire documentation of species loss, yet the political realities of negotiations, related to governments' economic interests, necessarily become embroiled in a range of dynamics that seems to frustrate all but the most apathetic. Furthermore, rarely are there opportunities to engage in a discussion of these root causes, particularly within the actual negotiations.

Though many activist CSOs have certainly maintained a presence in the corridors and meeting rooms of international policy negotiations, it is clear that many are disenchanted with what they perceive to be political obfuscation and intransigence of dominant governments. As the policy terrain transforms over time, government and non-governmental participants alike have raised significant concerns about the processes that unfold under UN-based deliberations. Some have gone so far as to question the utility of intergovernmental deliberations in the face of increasingly dire data regarding global environmental problems. Do we need the UN to negotiate policy? Is the 'least common denominator' result which is indicative of the consensus model of UN negotiating procedure adequate? What happens when powerful governments 'hijack' negotiations so that the end result is a policy that essentially has no 'teeth'? Many members of CSOs and IPOs articulate versions of these questions as they voice concerns related to the fact that the politics of the environment, as those politics are illuminated in UN negotiations, do not adequately represent the lived reality of individuals who experience the negative impact of global environmental degradation. From time to time, governments use this rhetoric to convey their interests. The impassioned plea from the lead negotiator for the government of Tuvalu to the delegations present at the 2009 UNFCCC COP15 in Copenhagen summarises this position: 'The entire population of Tuvalu lives below two metres above sea level ... We are not naïve to the circumstances and the political considerations that are before us.' However, in spite of the highly politicised dynamics that were bogging down negotiations at COP15, his intervention clearly argued that powerful governments 'should address the greatest threat to humanity that we have before us—climate change ... The fate of my country rests in your hands.'[3]

These concerns are not new. However, the ways in which they are being played out and the impact of the negotiations themselves on the dynamics that fuel these concerns merit academic analysis. In fact, Gale (2013) argues that current intergovernmentalism is incapable of delivering strong action on climate change. He posits that this is in part due to the fact that, in climate negotiations, 'the marginalisation of scientists, environmentalists, indigenous peoples and affected populations in small island states means that greater weight is placed on protecting short-term economic and social interests to the detriment of the planet's ecological future' (2013: 33). Gale's position parallels McKibben's in significant ways, in that both argue that the politics of negotiations fail to gel with the reality of human impact on the environment.

In many ways, I would reconfigure Gale's assertion to suggest that short-term economic interests—in fact, the very basis of most governments' economic interests—*serve to* marginalise scientists, environmentalists, and others whose critique calls into question the current hegemonic neoliberal economic order. In other words, as long as economic and not ecological dynamics remain central, scientists, environmentalists, and others who are critical of the root causes of environmental degradation will be marginalised by design.

Using examples from the negotiations, I investigate the ways in which participants navigate the inherent contradiction between what Schnaiberg (1980) has termed 'the treadmill of production' that organises the current global economy, and environmental sustainability. As both local and global economies are predominantly predicated on the imperative of growth (fairly narrowly defined by neoliberal economic theory), the discourse of sustainability raises merely rhetorical points as long as the fundamental economic order remains unchallenged. UN environmental negotiations provide very few spaces for this sort of analysis and thus are consigned to essentially 'rearranging the deck chairs on the Titanic', as participants remarked from time to time. CSOs and IPOs occasionally insert references to 'industry' more broadly, or to mining, energy, or agribusiness interests. Delegations who have achieved a critical stance towards the economic policies that have come to be known as the 'Washington Consensus'—such as Bolivia, or at times Ecuador and Venezuela—tend to take a fairly polemical position related to capitalism and market forces. Notwithstanding these cases, there is no room for robust discussions within the context of actual negotiations that tie the extractive, productive, and consumptive imperatives of the global economy (as it is currently structured) to environmental degradation. In fact, the very structure and purpose of negotiations, as they are organised around particular agenda items related to the process of deliberating the texts, preclude the possibility of discussion of root causes of environmental degradation. So, while 'science' has found its way into the lexicon of legitimate terrain for policy-makers to consider, the very nature of the imperative of economic growth upon which the current global economy is predicated is simply not up for discussion.

These themes thread throughout the specific examples of policy-making that comprise the focus of the substantive chapters of this book. My goal in this work is to explicate some of current dynamics that make up the terrain of UN-based policy-making by delving into specific policy-related issues that have emerged over the past few years, including deliberations regarding non-governmental participation in environmental negotiations, the science–policy interface in intergovernmental negotiations, the strategic use of language in policy negotiations, and the role of corporate interests in policy deliberations. While this is clearly not an exhaustive list of the dynamics that are of interest to CSOs and IPOs, each of these areas has emerged as being important to participants engaged in negotiations that have been taking place under the UNFCCC, CBD, UNPFII, and UNFF. To explore these dynamics, I utilise identifiable policy 'threads', as I have come to think of them, that emerged in actual negotiations that I observed. Attempting to follow a particular policy issue from one meeting to the next, I use these 'threads' as cases that are designed to elaborate on some of the larger theoretical discussions. Thus, while I focus my attention on the specific identified issue areas in order to give some specificity to the analysis and in order to be concrete about following various policy trajectories as they transformed during negotiations, and I regularly reference specific texts and actual situations that I observed, I simultaneously intend to contribute to larger theoretical and practical discussions that circumscribe these particular events.

Civil society in UN deliberations

A note on the term 'civil society' is merited, as it is a highly contested concept, both within and outside of the UN. There is a wide body of scholarship that has addressed the meaning, significance, and changing nature of civil society.[4] Subsequent chapters will address the complexity of civil society in greater detail where appropriate, although I do not endeavour to define the term in any definitive way. Instead, in the context of this particular study, the categorisation of 'civil society' is relevant to how it is that (literally) nongovernmental participants—meaning participants who are not credentialed on government delegations—enter into and engage in UN intergovernmental-policy deliberations. As the UN is first and foremost an *intergovernmental* organisation, those who access the negotiations must be government delegates or recognisable under an alternate yet institutionally-legitimised category. Currently, individuals who are not credentialed on government delegations access the UN through predetermined categories. For example, individuals who are not on government delegations access the UNFF as members of 'Major Groups'. The term 'Major Group' was codified in *Agenda 21: Earth Summit: The United Nations Program of Action from Rio* (UN 1993). The 'Major Groups' of participants (who are not delegates of nation-states) are defined as (1) Women, (2) Children and Youth, (3) Farmers, (4) Indigenous Peoples, (5) NGOs, (6) Trade Unions, (7) Local Authorities, (8) Science and Technology, and (9) Business and Industry. In negotiations that take place under the auspices of the Economic and Social Council (ECOSOC), each of these nine Major Groups serves as a possible entry point into the negotiations for individuals who are not on government delegations. Organisations that have consultative status with ECOSOC can credential participants for meetings of the bodies that fall under the bureaucratic umbrella of ECOSOC. This designation operates differently under the UNFCCC and CBD, as these bodies are positioned differently in the UN and therefore have different rules of procedure for vetting organisations through which participants can gain credentials to attend meetings. However, in each case there are predetermined categories of participation for non-governmental participants.

There is also a particular orientation to the policy process that is implied in my use of 'civil society' in this project. Many of the representatives of CSOs with whom I spoke exemplify what Florini (2000) terms 'the third force' in global politics: a transnational civil society which has a particular political orientation towards the policy processes in the sense that they see themselves as bringing important and perhaps neglected or underrepresented issues to the table. According to Florini, transnational civil society emerged as a third entity, with the nation-state and transnational or multinational corporations representing the other two forces (2000). My research, however, suggests that this is perhaps an outdated breakdown of global environmental governance in light of the current confluence of nation-state and corporate interests. In fact, scholars who take a critical stance towards neoliberalism have analysed the key intersections between nation-states and corporations in the building up of the current hegemonic world order, particularly in the time period after the Second World War to the present. As CSOs critique the influence of corporate interests on government delegates' negotiating positions, they often see themselves as providing fundamental representation in the debates for those who are marginalised by the workings of global capitalism in a neoliberal economic age. Johnson, in her analysis of the role of NGOs in the negotiations of the Nonproliferation and Test Ban Treaty, highlights the dynamic associated with the 'revolving door in U.S. politics, which allows academics, lawyers, and diplomats to be in key governmental positions one day and back in their universities or nongovernmental institutions the next' (2000: 69). It is not unusual for people with what is deemed to be relevant expertise to be seconded to government delegations for particular meetings. Increasingly, legal expertise is required on government delegations, either to handle the complexities of international law (in terms of intellectual property, for example, in the negotiations associated with the CBD), or to facilitate in the wordsmithing to ensure that agreements represent the position that governments intend them to (it was rumoured that the United States had thirty-four lawyers on its delegation to the UNFCCC COP21 in Paris). Including individuals on government delegations who have expertise related to corporate interests has become increasingly prevalent as the web of Multilateral Environmental Agreements (MEAs) becomes more complex and, often, overlapping in mandates. To Johnson's observation I would add that this multiplicity of roles is clearly not unique to the United States, nor is it insignificant when looking specifically at which roles are played and by whom. The major players in international economic fora such as the World Trade Organisation (WTO) or World Economic Forum (WEF), for example, are increasingly chosen to represent government interests based on their experience of an increasingly blurred boundary between government and corporate interests. I note this because it represents an important dynamic in terms of the constitution of the current configuration of 'civil society'. In many ways, rather than representing an important 'third force' in global politics, transnational CSOs often represent a counterforce, in constant negotiation with (and increasingly in opposition to) government/corporate interests. As I will address in more detail in my concluding chapter, the emergence within UN negotiations of the discourse of 'public–private partnerships', 'payments for ecosystem services', and a 'green economy' among other examples of the language of marketisation represents the broader terrain that exists beyond the walls of UN negotiations yet permeates and organises these deliberations in many ways. Not only are there often concerns that agreements made in economic fora (such as the WTO) trump the agreements that can be made in environmental negotiations, but the broader exigencies of economic systems, as I mentioned earlier, that are predicated on neoliberal premises define the terms of the debate in ways that are often anathema to CSO and IPO goals.

It should be clear that my use of the term CSO is informed by the debates within non-governmental (non-state) actors' groups as it is also informed by my interest in highlighting the strategic work done by those who contest dominant discourses. This is to say that it does not make sense to argue that all CSOs are activist, pro-nature, and anti-capitalist. However, there is often what I see as an 'activist' component to civil society participation in environmental negotiations that deserves analysis, as they are the participants who see themselves as being present for 'damage control' or 'holding governments' feet to the fire'.[5] In fact, seasoned CSOs recognise that, to be effective, they must speak in terms that can be incorporated into (and recognised by) the frameworks established within the institutional discourse, or find themselves disenfranchised from the negotiations. While this does not render them completely without agency, my work speaks specifically to the ways in which this process of framing the debate, disenfranchising non-compliant actors, and redefining formerly progressive interests to make them non-threatening to the dominant discourse actually works within the context of the UN.

Finally, it is important to note that, while the UN-designated civil society categories often include Indigenous Peoples as technically non-governmental, in my analysis I often distinguish civil society participants from 'Indigenous Peoples' participants due to the fact that, based on the premises of sovereignty and self-determination that are central to Indigenous Peoples' participation in UN fora and elsewhere (see, for example, Dahl 2012; Eastwood 2011; and Pritchard 1998), it is not appropriate to designate Indigenous Peoples as falling under the auspices of civil society which implies a distinctly *non*-governmental status. In other words, while Indigenous Peoples are included in many of the official designations of 'civil society' established by the various UN bodies, multiple participants recognise that this is problematic due to the fact that one of the key concerns of Indigenous Peoples is that their identity as peoples precedes the current system of nation-states that organises the UN as an institution. In contrast to the position of many current nation-states, I work here with the premise that

Indigenous Peoples constitute legitimate governments that should be addressed as such in spite of the fact that they have been colonised, subjected to genocide, disregarded, or dispossessed by nation-states. Thus, Indigenous Peoples attempt to negotiate the tensions caused by this 'non-governmental' designation in a variety of different ways.

What a 'sociological imagination' brings to global environmental governance

My analysis in this book is predicated on the fundamental sociological premise that individual human activities in specific locations are organised by larger social relations. I have referenced the term 'sociological imagination' as C.W. Mills (1959) intended, to develop just what it is that sociologists bring to the table in terms of our disciplinary analytical orientation. Mills defines the sociological imagination as 'the quality of mind essential to grasp the interplay of man [sic] and society, of biography and history, of self and world' (1959: 4). While 'the facts of history are also facts about individual men and women' (Mills 1959: 3), 'the sociological imagination enables us to grasp history and biography and the relations between the two' (1959: 6). Mills uses Marx's notion of history not simply to speak to events that have happened in the past but more to mean the broader web of social relations that serve as a context for each of our individual experiences. To elaborate, the idea is to see the individual 'subject' not as an end point to our investigation but instead as a vector into the workings of larger social relations. Here I mean 'social relations' to include a range of organising dynamics, from norms of interpersonal interaction, to the codified bureaucratic rules of document production, to larger discursive and ideological contexts whereby 'common sense', or the 'taken-for-granted' (Bannerji 1995; Gramsci 1971; Ridzi 2009). This includes hegemonic understandings which are organised by current discourses in important ways such as how economies are intended to work (the 'Washington Consensus') or what 'development' means, for example (McMichael 2012). This is not a deterministic framework, as social relations are generated within the context of human social organisation—and therefore can be contested and transformed. However, 'relations of ruling' or 'ruling relations' (Smith 1999) organise human behaviour in significant ways, making anti-hegemonic options less viable or even less visible. For Smith, '[t]he concept of ruling relations identifies an historical development of forms of social consciousness that can no longer be adequately conceived as arising in the life conditions of actual individuals' (1999: 78). Instead of being merely representative of an amalgamation of individual experiences, the concept of ruling relations 'directs investigation to a complex of objectified relations, coordinating the activities of many, many people whose consciousness as subjects is formed within those relations' (Smith 1999: 78). This 'coordinating' function of relations of ruling is key. The role of the researcher, then, is to explicate the workings of these ruling relations by way of illustrating how individuals within the institution being investigated (in this case, the UN) navigate the extant terrain and orient themselves to the work that they do—as that work is coordinated extra-locally—in ways that are not of their choosing. From this perspective, individuals, as they engage in their work, illuminate the ruling relations that circumscribe and organise that work. Following this framework, rather than to speak theoretically about 'bureaucracy', 'globalisation' or 'neoliberalism', my interest is instead in using the actual activities of individuals who are engaged in policy processes as a means of exploring the larger social relations that serve to organise the world of policy work—as it is made by actual people in specific locations.

In analysing the social relations that frame what goes on in UN negotiations, I argue that other fora, such as the WTO, World Intellectual Property Organization (WIPO), the WEF, or meetings of the G8 and G20 constitute significant nodes in the generation of a discursive terrain upon which debates about climate, biological diversity, access to genetic resources, civil society, Indigenous rights, access to technology, and other such relevant matters must occur. The large intergovernmental bodies, many of which are far less accessible to members of civil society, have significant connections to each other beyond the construction of the discursive terrain. For example, the 2015 meetings of the G20 in Turkey, just prior to the Paris UN climate negotiations, were primarily organised around discussions of economic growth yet also grappled with how the G20 governments were going to address climate commitments at the Paris meetings. As my project concerns itself with elucidating the connections between the everyday world of environmental policy-making and the relations of ruling that circumscribe that world, explicating the components of those larger relations of ruling—for example, the discourses that organise the global economy—will be one of the elements I develop as I engage in my analysis of specific negotiations.

'UN-conventional' methods: Observation, participation, and document analysis

For scholarship on international environmental governance, this book is somewhat eclectic in terms of its approach to international environmental policy. I have chosen to draw on a range of methods to gather my data as those allow me to address what I find to be the most interesting questions about the UN as an institution and global environmental governance as a phenomenon. As a sociologist, while I find alternative perspectives useful and fruitful, I largely eschew theories that emanate from the fields of political science or international relations and rarely engage in debates in ways that are conventional to those disciplines. Falling broadly under the rubric of qualitative sociological research, as I mentioned earlier, I approached my data-gathering ethnographically in that I observed UN meetings in various locations around the globe. This needs some elaboration, as Harper notes that the term 'ethnography' can be used by anthropologists and sociologists as 'a catch-all phrase for a range of different things, just as long as they involve field work of some sort or another' (1998: 49). In the case of my research, rather than being theory-driven, my data collection has been organised around observing and documenting the work (broadly defined) of individuals who are engaged in policy-making under the auspices of the UN. Ethnography as a methodology allows for the collection of rich, descriptive, qualitative data. However, like many ethnographers, I am not interested only in describing these processes. As Smith writes, unlike with quantitative research methods, '[t]he ethnographer is not looking for agreement among different informants but for the intersections and complementarities of their different accounts in the relations that coordinate their work' (2005: 63). Here we see the relevance of the 'sociological imagination' discussed earlier, in the sense that individuals provide opportunities for the researcher to investigate the larger context that circumscribes their work. The emphasis on the 'relations' that serve to coordinate peoples' work is fundamentally sociological in nature. Individuals, as they navigate the complex and constantly shifting terrain of policy, provide opportunities for insights into how larger social relations serve to coordinate the world of policy.

In the chapters that follow, as I develop the cases I have identified and elaborate on the specific policy trajectories, I explore some of the tensions and implications of the policy processes on which I focus. This analysis, while not claiming to solve environmental policy problems, is intended to contribute to a better understanding of the complexity of 'environmental governance'—a phrase that has become very much in vogue—as it plays itself out (or, more accurately, as it is played out by active, knowledgeable individuals) in specific locations where policy is made. The analysis also highlights the institutional constraints and organisation of the UN itself—constraints that are both structural and normative in nature.

The overall goal in using the methods I have selected is to work towards concretising abstract and theoretical notions related to 'global governance' and 'civil society' by elucidating the actual work of members of CSOs and IPOs, and, where relevant, other participants, as those participants have attempted to influence policy processes. While there are models for sociological and anthropological work that analyse the workings of institutions with global reach (see, for example, Ferguson 1994, 2006; Goldman 2005; Harper 1998; Li 2007; Mosse 2005), and I encountered other ethnographers during portions of my fieldwork in the meetings of the UN, as I mentioned above, phenomena associated with international policy tend to be analysed by those in disciplines associated with political science and international relations. A perusal of the published research on 'global governance' indicates a marked increase in interest in the topic by scholars in these fields over the past few years. However, we know that, as researchers, we select our methods based upon what sorts of questions we are interested in asking, and, likewise, what sort of dynamics we are compelled to investigate. For McDermott, Levin and Cashore, the 'mainstream theories within international relations (IR) and public policy that focus on the role of institutions and subsystems are unable to explain long-term logics of deforestation and degradation that have more to do with global capitalism and consumption' (2011: 86). Therefore, for these scholars, and for my own analysis, deploying a methodology that incorporates the possibility of analysing the connections between institutions, individual actions, and global capitalism is crucial. Likewise, Lapegna (2009) notes that sociological and anthropological studies of global phenomena bring different perspectives to the table than those based within the disciplinary theories of international relations or political economy. For Lapegna, the methods used in anthropology or sociology can help address the critique that political economic treatments of global phenomena can be overly deterministic in the sense that the theoretical models serve to subsume individual activities. Litfin, too, has set her work apart from some of the assumptions imbedded in the theoretical frameworks of disciplines that concern themselves with international relations. According to Litfin, 'conventional approaches to international relations tend to depict power as a material resource, a tool wielded by nation-states to further their own interests' (1998: 2); however, 'reflectivist approaches', such as those that Litfin uses to analyse the discourses that organised the Montreal Protocol process, allow researchers to 'understand policy-making as a problem-solving activity with important intersubjective dimensions' (Litfin 1998: 4). Indeed, this intersubjective dimension is represented in my work as I develop what it means for individuals to deploy their sophisticated work knowledges in order to strategically engage in the policy-making processes.

Additionally, as discussed in this chapter, I argue that it is crucial to place the UN within the context of a globalised economy, as I work from the premise that environmental degradation, as well as the policies designed to address environmental problems, are intricately interwoven with larger economic trends, including an increased marketisation of the environment and the exigencies of consumption in economies that are predicated on growth-based capitalism. I therefore approached the UN not with the goal of identifying 'best practices' or measuring NGO impact on policy processes, as others have done (see, for example, Betsill and Corell 2001; Gunter 2004; Humphreys 2004). While this is critical and timely work, my project provides a different contribution to this literature. I am intrigued by questions related to the 'how' of policy-making—*how* it actually works in practice, and what larger translocal dynamics (such as those predicated on the necessity to maintain the 'treadmill of production') serve to organise those practices and policy outcomes. My aim here in this book is not to call into question the premises on which other disciplines are based but instead to argue that complex dynamics require multidisciplinary perspectives. As a relative methodological outlier in the field of global environmental govern-ance, I do not wish to downplay the significance of other disciplines' approaches to the arenas with which I engage. Instead, as my approach is somewhat unconventional, my goal is to clearly state what it is I am attempting to contribute to the debate, lest readers' expectations differ. In following specific policy-related threads, and applying qualitative, ethnographically based research methods in gathering data, I hope to contribute an alternative yet complementary angle of analysis.

Using this lens, it was important for me to orient to the work that participants, particularly those who represented CSOs and IPOs, did to become knowledgeable about the issues and specific texts/documents as those texts and issues were being negotiated. Furthermore, I focused on the ways in which these participants strategically worked to influence the various policy processes I observed. Dorothy Smith frames it this way: 'Institutional ethnography's modest proposal is to work from what people are doing or what they can tell us about what they and others do and to find out how the forms of coordinating their activities 'produce' institutional processes, as they actually work' (2005: 60). 'For institu-tional ethnography, the social as the focus for study is to be located in how people's activities or practices are *coordinated*' (Smith 2005: 59, emphasis in the original). Clearly, this discussion illuminates the fact that research method is 'more than a collection of research techniques and procedural guidelines. It's orienting to the world' (Gubrium and Holstein 1997: vii). In simple terms, Smith states the overarching ontology of institutional ethnography as follows:

> Institutional ethnography's program is one of inquiry and discovery. It has no prior interpretive commitment such as that which follows from concepts such as *global domination* or *resistance*. It means to find out just how people's doings in the everyday are articulated to and coordinated by extended social relations that are not visible from within any particular local setting and just how people are participating in those relations.
>
> (2005: 36, italics in the original)

As Grahame and Grahame write, institutional ethnography emphasises '(1) ethnography as an approach to studying social organisation and (2) a conception of institutional processes in which text-based forms of coordination play a key role' (2012: 1). The primacy of the text in UN negotiations, in some ways, makes institutional ethnography an apt approach. Within the context of the negotiations I observed, while texts are ever present, they do not appear as 'forms' that need to be filled out (with the exception of the process of credentialing participants for access to negotiations). Instead, they appear as policy briefs, negotiating texts, 'white papers', 'non-papers', Declarations, Agreements, Accords, and the like. They organise individuals' actions in ways that I will elaborate on in subsequent chapters, but they are also manifestations of larger ruling relations that likewise serve to organise what goes on inside the UN. Richard Harper's (1998) approach to his research on the International Monetary Fund (IMF) is useful here. As Harper immersed himself as an ethnographer in the policy-laden work of IMF bureaucrats, he too focused on 'the organization of the organization' in order 'to draw attention to how the Fund organizes itself to do certain tasks' (1998: 111). Influenced by the centrality of texts in Dorothy Smith's work, Harper examines both the textually mediated nature of the IMF as an institution as well as the background knowledge that practitioners need to have in order to activate texts within work processes. Harper's methodological device of 'following the information career' (1998: 70) within the IMF allowed him to track particular documents as they made their way through the organisation— not in a random or unpredictable fashion but in a manner that was clearly 'organised' by—and that clearly served to organise—work processes in the IMF. For Harper, seeing 'information' as having a 'career', and as doing particular work, is a crucial manner of accessing the workings of the institution being studied. This technique allows for the researcher to develop a certain focus without losing sight of the larger dynamics that provide the context for that information. Organisations such as the IMF (or in my case the UN) are extremely complex and confound the typical 'site' orientation that many ethnographers adopt. Tracking the 'information career', or, in my case, particular policy trajectories or 'threads', allows one to navigate through the organisation and to illuminate the work that practitioners do to strategically intervene in particular processes. I found the UN deliberations I studied to be many-headed beasts with seemingly endless threads of policy transformations. In my case, the selection of particular issues that became salient to CSOs and IPOs allowed me to follow particular threads in a relatively manageable manner—to maintain an ethnographic focus, yet to do so within the context of a highly unconventional site in traditional ethnographic terms.

'Text work': Analysis of a documentary reality

Contemporary scholars have clearly theorised 'text' as a phenomenon worthy of analysis. However, for Smith, 'it is important to hang on to the association of words or images with some definite material form that is capable of replication. It is the *replicability of texts* that substructs the ruling relations; replicability is a condition of their existence' (2005: 166, italics in original). It is clear that texts organise the work of policy participants in significant ways within UN-based negotiations. While it is true that texts organise peoples' work in many professions, the negotiation of text is a particular type of 'text work' that I analyse in the context of UN negotiations. In Chapter 2, I provide more details on the ways in which negotiations actually work in order to provide readers with a context for my analysis. This text work is clearly tied to the larger discourses or 'conceptual currency' of the institution. 'Institutional discourses are central to the coordinating of the work that people do in bringing into being every day the institutional complexes embedded in the ruling relations' (Smith 2005: 111). The documents produced within UN deliberations have a particular character. Thus, in analysing specific negotiations, I have included actual texts in order to illustrate how it is that language is negotiated, contested, and ultimately codified within the documents themselves. This book takes up the strategic work that is organised around producing the UN documentary reality, which includes the production of the documents themselves along with the production of the discursive terrain that then serves to organise future deliberations. In mapping out how certain language is brought into various negotiations, I have, where relevant, linked this language to participants' interests. In this way, the work that becomes largely invisible in the 'final' texts is made visible again in my analysis—as strategic work that is designed to ensure that participants' interests are represented in the outcomes of the negotiations.

Plus ça change…

Here, I feel compelled to state some caveats. In taking on a project related to ongoing policy processes, I have set my work up to be, in some ways, obsolete by the time it goes to press. In fact, while I have incorporated some contemporary information related to these specific policy threads, the reality is that the cases I have chosen to follow are constantly transforming. In fact, during one of the edits of these chapters, the Bonn meetings of the UNFCCC, including the forty-fourth sessions of the Subsidiary Body for Implementation (SBI44) and the Subsidiary Body for Scientific and Technological Advice (SBSTA44), and the first meeting of the Ad-Hoc Working Group on the Paris Agreement (APA1) were taking place. It has been a challenge to ignore email notifications about the deliberations, as they are surely relevant to the themes I analyse in this book. The pace of change in policy debates, the nature of ethnographic research, availability of funding, the exigencies of my academic position—all have created a particular dynamic whereby the cases I develop are immediately outdated as soon as I exit the research site, and my plans to re-enter the research site are constantly in the making. This is not the traditional framework of research where data are gathered, analysis ensues, followed by writing. Instead, there has been considerable back-and-forth, with forays into the field, and with difficult decisions to simply stop researching in order to actually make progress with writing. While this has caused significant consternation for me, and those engaged in the everyday work related to these policy trends will inevitably see the gaps in my analysis, the research is intended to take a snapshot of events as they are played out in identifiable locations with the goal of illustrating key dynamics that transcend the specific cases used in analysis here. In other words, readers who are hoping to gain the most cutting-edge updates on 'Loss and Damage' under the UNFCCC, for example, will be sorely disappointed. Not only has it not been practical for me to become highly knowledgeable about any one of the negotiating fora, but my goal has been to shed a broader light on the making of policy by using specific examples to illustrate how it is that the work of policy deliberations actually gets done. In fact, while this book is intended to highlight certain policy-making processes, those who are entangled in policy processes to a much more significant degree than I am will inevitably know far more about the specific

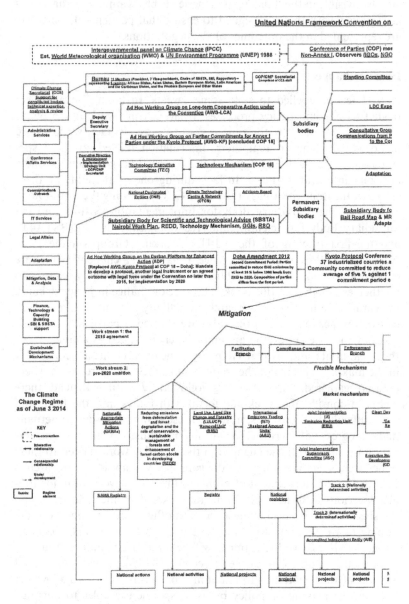

Figure 1.1 Organogram of the Climate Change Regime.
Reproduced with permission of Dr Timothy Cadman.

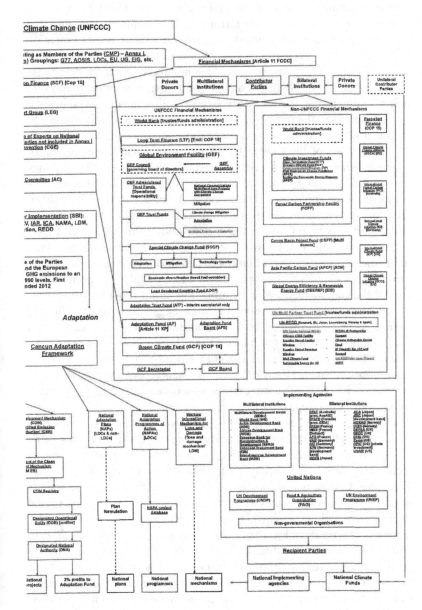

Figure 1.1 (Cont.)

rationale behind decisions, the actual events that transpired that served to cause shifts in the discursive terrain, and the political exigencies that undergird particular governments' positions. Based on my participation in the processes as a researcher, I have followed the investigative methods of the ethnographer—investigating hunches and probing for details. As an academic who has harboured a bit of an obsession for seemingly dull policy dialogues for decades now, I can recall moments of excitement as participants in the policy processes revealed to me what it was like to be present in closed meetings, such as those that took place in the most turbulent hours of the COP15 UNFCCC meetings in Copenhagen, for example, when significant events transpired that shaped future policy outcomes. Those experiences also revealed to me how little I could possibly ever know about the entire scope of the policy arenas I have taken on as my research sites. Given the sheer scope of policy transformations and trajectories in any *one* of the specific bodies through which I have conducted my research, I have often reflected on the utter folly of taking on a research project that attempts to develop 'expertise' in several of those bodies. Some scholars spend their careers analysing specific elements of the climate regime, for example. Figure 1.1 provides an example of the ways in which Timothy Cadman began to map the climate-change regime. Ultimately, he created an interactive web-based model that includes even more complexity than is represented in Figure 1.1.[6] The hardcover version of Yamin and Depledge's 2004 tome entitled *The International Climate Change Regime: A Guide to Rules, Institutions, and Procedures* is 730 pages long, and by now is missing 14 years of transformations that have taken place since its publication.

However, I have regularly been fascinated with the dynamics that thread through the various negotiating processes. Indeed, the very work of what it means to become a skilled UN negotiator—whether government delegate or civil society representative—is worthy of attention. Therefore, I claim neither to be articulating the final (or most recent) word on the policies I analyse, nor to be an 'expert' in any one of the international regimes in which I have conducted my fieldwork. The policy terrain is far too complex, the issues are in a constant state of change, and, while there are landmark decisions and Declarations, and while particular powerful nations make dramatic shows of withdrawing from the Kyoto Protocol, the Paris Agreement and even the Human Rights Council, there appears to be no specific end in sight for UN negotiations.

Likewise, in an effort to maintain readability for a non-policy-entrenched audience, I have opted, in some cases, to simplify or intentionally gloss over some of the more technical elements of the negotiations. Some of this has been done in an effort to reduce the alphabet-soup nature of UN-related topics as much as possible while still attempting to retain enough information as to be true to the substance of the negotiations. This is in part related to my observation that, when I have had opportunities to present this research over the past several years, my audience tends to get lost in acronyms to the detriment of the analysis I intend to make. The following example illustrates this dynamic: The Fifteenth Conference of Parties of the UNFCCC was technically the COP15/MOP5 (Fifteenth Conference of Parties to the UNFCCC/Fifth Meeting of Parties to the Kyoto Protocol). It was also the thirty-first session of the Subsidiary Body for Implementation (SBI) and the Subsidiary Body for Scientific and Technological Advice (SBSTA), the tenth session of the Ad-Hoc Working Group on Further Commitments for Annex I Parties under the Kyoto Protocol (AWG-KP), and the eighth session of the Ad-Hoc Working Group on Long-Term Cooperative Action under the Convention (AWG-LCA). This need not be so confusing for the purposes I am attempting to accomplish in this book. Seasoned negotiators and policy-makers may rankle at my shorthand manner of presenting the details, but I have made several editorial choices for the purposes of allowing the research to be readable for a range of audiences.

Lastly, I have made the choice to retain some degree of repetition in the various chapters in the event that readers are interested in using individual chapters as stand-alone entities. Whereas some chapters are designed to explain particular elements in greater detail, my goal has been to allow each chapter to function as a relatively self-contained unit at the same time as it contributes to the larger goals of the manuscript as a whole. This is a difficult balance, as I run the risk of alienating readers who read the entire manuscript in repeating some key acronyms and explanations. However, I trust that the skimming skills we have learned as academics can be put to use in these cases as the larger goal of allowing each chapter to more or less stand on its own has been important to me throughout the writing of this book.

Chapters

In this first chapter, my objective has been to set up my broader project— what it is that I am attempting to accomplish in this book, along with identifying some of the things that I am *not* attempting to take on. Given the methodology, I argue that it is important to give the reader some glimpses of the world of policy negotiations at the same time as I have attempted to frame the complexity of the dynamics associated with this world. Here, through the ethnographically derived 'snippets' and the framing of how things actually work in practice, I have intended to provide a context for subsequent chapters by noting the types of questions and concerns that orient my project to the UN as a research site. Through a description of the methodology that has informed data collection and analysis, the chapter makes the argument that a focus on the *practice* of global governance allows the researcher to tie somewhat theoretical concepts to actual activities of the practitioners who negotiate policy, without losing sight of the larger social relations that serve to organise the negotiations. The issues raised that are related to democratic decision-making, competing national and global interests, the intersections of global economic concerns with environmental policy, and the relationship between science, technology, and policy thread throughout the chapters.

Chapter 2 introduces unfamiliar readers to the workings of the UN. In addition, it orients familiar readers with the specific elements of the UN that are relevant to my analysis. Non-governmental participants who engage in UN negotiations realise that their contributions to the process are contingent on their ability to work within the structural and ideological constraints of the UN organisational complex. However, the strategies that participants deploy to effectively engage in the processes demonstrate that global environmental governance is not a vague and abstract entity but is instead generated through the actions of specific individuals in actual locations—with implications for situated individuals who may have no contact with UN deliberations. Chapter 2 sets up the 'site' in terms of its relevant components for what it is I am trying to accomplish in this broader analysis.

Chapters 3 and 4 are substantive chapters in the sense that they focus on dynamics that have been identified by members of CSOs and IPOs as having particular topical significance. The chapters are structured so that each delves into a particular point in the history of a specific policy event. Chapter 3, for example, takes a look at a specific set of issues that became salient immediately following the landmark 2009 Copenhagen climate conference. Thus, we are taken to a historical example of climate negotiation to investigate the sorts of dynamics that become relevant for stakeholders. Based on specific dynamics that unfolded at UNFCCC meetings in Bonn in 2010, I bring readers in to the negotiations by highlighting some of the positions taken by governments and by members of CSOs. Ultimately, the dynamics that took place at the meeting from which I draw my examples speak to larger conflicts between policy and science *and* between civil society and governments. I investigate various forms of activism, and note the activist–policy disjuncture.

The case of policy negotiation that is highlighted in Chapter 4 involves the ways in which biotechnology has emerged as being salient to the negotiations of the CBD. I investigate the disjuncture between scientific advancements and the policy negotiations which has created a circumstance where negotiators have had to wrestle with how—or whether—to advocate for regulations on emerging technologies. In this chapter, I delve into a particular series of negotiations in order to develop a sense of how participants attempt to influence policy outcomes. Additionally, I look at the larger debates that circumscribe those specific negotiations to investigate the ways in which biotechnology represents a fascinating case for environmental policy due to its scientific complexity and its legal implications. Biotechnology also exists as a 'cross-cutting' issue with implications for UN bodies other than the CBD.

Chapter 5 returns explicitly to the argument I make here in Chapter 1 regarding the disjuncture between the exigencies of the current global economy and the environmental problems that the UN bodies are designed to address. In essence, given the imperatives for economic growth that are built into the global economy, governments come to the table with highly conflicting mandates. The chapter provides examples of circumstances where CSOs and IPOs sought to bring a critique of capitalism into the debates and the ways in which 'agenda items' are not designed for this sort of discussion. As long as economic growth reigns supreme as both national and global primary goals, the debates about environmental degradation will merely act as a substitute for actual action to curb environmental harm. Many members of CSOs and IPOs recognise this disjuncture yet find few opportunities within the context of actual UN negotiations to voice or address this concern. I conclude that the very structure of UN deliberations, which fails to address the exigencies of the current global economy, precludes the possibility of genuinely addressing the ultimate root cause of environmental degradation.

Notes

1 A substantial amount of the data for this book were collected with the support of a Social Science Research Council Abe Fellowship from 2009 to 2011. However, I have been observing UN-based negotiations since 1998 and continued to attend meetings for research purposes after 2011 (throughout the completion of this manuscript). I have thus included data from the full range of research (1998 to 2018) where appropriate. Since 1998, I have attended forty-four meetings that have taken place under the auspices of the United Nations, including conferences of Parties, ad-hoc Working Groups, expert groups, and other meetings designed to inform UN negotiations.

2 Field notes COP16, Cancun (29 November, 2010).

3　Statement made by Ian Fry, lead negotiator for Tuvalu, to the UNFCCC COP15, Copenhagen, Denmark. Saturday, 12 December 2009.
4　See Eastwood 2013 for a discussion of the various branches of this scholarship.
5　I originally attribute these phrases to Bill Mankin, who was a prominent and active contributor to NGO participation in the forest policy negotiations throughout my dissertation research (IFF meetings). I have since heard these very phrases repeated quite regularly by other non-governmental participants, particularly when I have asked them why they continue to participate in UN policy processes in spite of their frustrations and the clear message that the outcomes of the policy processes are not what they would want.
6　Dr Timothy Mark Cadman's interactive map of the climate regime can be accessed here: http://climateregimemap.net/

References

Bannerji, H. (1995) *Thinking Through: Essays on Feminism, Marxism and Anti-Racism*, Toronto: Women's Press.
Betsill, M. and E. Corell (2001) 'NGO Influence in International Environmental Negotiations: A Framework for Analysis', *Global Environmental Politics*, 1(4): 86–107.
Dahl, J. (2012) *The Indigenous Space and Marginalized People in the United Nations*, New York: Palgrave Macmillan.
Eastwood, L.E. (2011) 'Resisting Dispossession: Indigenous Peoples, the World Bank, and the Contested Terrain of Policy', *New Global Studies*, 5(1): 1–33.
—— (2013) 'Civil Society', *Oxford Bibliographies*, New York: Oxford University Press, available at www.oxfordbibliographies.com/view/document/obo-9780199756384/obo-9780199756384-0148.xml (accessed 21 September 2018).
Ferguson, J. (1994) *The Anti-Politics Machine: 'Development', Depoliticization, and Bureaucratic Power in Lesotho*, Minneapolis, MN: University of Minnesota Press.
—— (2006) *Global Shadows: Africa in the Neoliberal World Order*, Durham, NC: Duke University Press.
Florini, A.M. (ed.) (2000) *The Third Force: The Rise of Transnational Civil Society*, Washington, DC: Carnegie Endowment for International Peace.
Gale, F. (2013) 'When Interests Trump Institutions: Tasmania's Forest Policy Network and the Bell Bay Pulp Mill', *Environmental Politics*, 22(2): 274–92.
Goldman, M. (2005) *Imperial Nature: The World Bank and Struggles for Social Justice in the Age of Globalization*, New Haven, CT: Yale University Press.
Grahame, P.R. and K.M. Grahame (2012) 'Institutional Ethnography', in G. Ritzer (ed.), *Blackwell Encyclopedia of Sociology*, Oxford: Blackwell Publishing.
Gramsci, A. (1971) *Selections from the Prison Notebooks*, New York: International Publisher's Co.

Gubrium, J. and J. Holstein (1997) *The New Language of Qualitative Method*, Oxford: Oxford University Press.

Gunter, M.M., Jr. (2004) *Building the Next Ark: How NGOs Work to Protect Biodiversity*, Hanover, NH: Dartmouth College Press.

Hansen, James, Makiko Sato, Pushker Kharecha, David Beerling, Robert Berner, Valerie Masson-Delmotte, Mark Pagani, Maureen Raymo, Dana L. Royer, James C. Zachos (2008) 'Target Atmospheric CO_2: Where Should Humanity Aim?' *Open Atmospheric Science Journal*, 2: 217–31.

Harper, R. (1998) *Inside the IMF: An Ethnography of Documents, Technology and Organisational Action*, Orlando, FL: Academic Press Inc.

Harriss, J. (2002) *Depoliticizing Development: The World Bank and Social Capital*, London: Anthem Press.

Humphreys, D. (1996) *Forest Politics: The Evolution of International Cooperation*, London: Earthscan.

—— (2004) 'Redefining the Issues: NGO Influence on International Forest Negotiations', *Global Environmental Politics*, 4(2): 51–74.

—— (2006) *Logjam: Deforestation and the Crisis of Global Governance*, London: Earthscan.

Intergovernmental Platform on Biodiversity and Ecosystem Services (IPBES) (n.d.) *About: What Is IPBES?* available at www.ipbes.net/about-ipbes.html (accessed 16 September 2016).

IPCC (2014) *Climate Change 2014: Impacts, Adaptation, and Vulnerability. Part A: Global and Sectoral Aspects. Contribution of Working Group II to the Fifth Assessment Report of the Intergovernmental Panel on Climate Change*, Cambridge: Cambridge University Press.

Johnson, R. (2000) 'Advocates and Activists: Conflicting Approaches on Nonproliferation and the Test Ban Treaty', in A.M. Florini (ed.), *The Third Force: The Rise of Transnational Civil Society*, Washington, DC: Carnegie Endowment for International Peace, pp. 49–82.

Lapegna, P. (2009) 'Ethnographers of the World ... United? Current Debates on the Ethnographic Study of 'Globalization'', *Journal of World-Systems Research*, 15(1): 3–24.

Li, T.M. (2007) *The Will to Improve: Governmentality, Development, and the Practice of Politics*, Durham, NC: Duke University Press.

Litfin, K. (1998) *The Greening of Sovereignty in World Politics*, Cambridge, MA: MIT Press.

McDermott, C.L., K. Levin, and B. Cashore (2011) 'Building the Forest-Climate Bandwagon: REDD+ and the Logic of Problem Amelioration', *Global Environmental Politics*, 11(3): 85–103.

McKibben, B. (2015) 'Climate Deal: The Pistol Has Fired, So Why Aren't We Running?' *The Guardian*, 13 December, available at www.theguardian.com/commentisfree/2015/dec/13/paris-climate-talks-15c-marathon-negotiating-physics (accessed 28 December 2015).

McMichael, P. (2012) *Development and Social Change: A Global Perspective*, Thousand Oaks, CA: Sage Publications.

Mills, C.W. (1959) *The Sociological Imagination*, Oxford: Oxford University Press.

Mosse, D. (2005) *Cultivating Development: An Ethnography of Aid Policy and Practice*, London: Pluto Press.

Pritchard, S. (ed.) (1998) *Indigenous People, the United Nations, and Human Rights*, Sydney: Zed Books, Ltd.

Ridzi, F. (2009) *Selling Welfare Reform: Work-First and the New Common Sense of Employment*, New York: New York University Press.

Schnaiberg, A. (1980) *The Environment: From Surplus to Scarcity*, Oxford: Oxford University Press.

Smith, D.E. (1999) *Writing the Social: Critique, Theory, and Investigations*, Toronto: University of Toronto Press.

—— (2005) *Institutional Ethnography: A Sociology for People*, Oxford: Alta Mira Press.

United Nations Environment Program (UNEP) (1993) *Agenda 21: Earth Summit—The United Nations Programme of Action from Rio*. New York: UN.

United Nations (n.d.) *The United Nations at a Glance*, available at https://web.archive.org/web/20141225170544/www.un.org/en/aboutun/index.shtml (accessed 5 January 2015).

Yamin, F. and J. Depledge (2004) *The International Climate Change Regime: A Guide to Rules, Institutions, and Procedures*, Cambridge: Cambridge University Press.

2 Setting the scene
The UN as an ethnographic research site

In order to be effective you need to speak to the Agenda ... what governments really want to hear is agreed language. Are your policy aims feasible? These are things you need to assess if you want to engage in the process.

(Civil Society Workshop on the UN 'Zero Draft':
presentation on civil society engagement in the
UN Rio+20 process, field notes, 24 January 2012)

Introduction: 'Ethnographic snippet' to set the scene

The bus lurches through morning rush-hour traffic in Miraflores, just outside of Lima, Peru. Each seat is occupied, although the seat next to mine holds the backpack of a man who is standing in the aisle conferring with several of his colleagues. Even the time it takes to be transported to meetings is precious for participants engaging in the meetings held by the UNFCCC. I can't help but notice that the 'Tourismo' transportation that has been provided by the host government of Peru is worlds above the crowded minibus transportation taking Lima locals to work today. Filled with UNFCCC COP20 participants, each of us identifiable by the baby-blue lanyard from which dangles our access badge, the bus commute to the venue is not a quiet time of contemplation or mental preparation for the day. I may well be the only lone traveller not discussing the most recent draft text with my colleagues seated around me. Instead, I'm furiously taking field notes to capture this as one of the arenas where the work of policy-making gets done.

One woman is turned in her seat with her head craned around in order to talk to the man behind her. I hear him say, 'You'll note that the last paragraph contains the language ...' Between the din of other conversations in a variety of languages and the rumble of the motor, I'm unable to catch the substance of their conversation, but it is clear that they are discussing recent drafts of negotiating texts—most likely texts that were distributed late the night before or in the early hours of the morning. My would-be seatmate, rather than sitting next to me, spends the entire 45-minute commute strategising with his colleagues about recent texts and what to anticipate in today's negotiations.

Based on my experience at four separate UNFCCC COPs prior to Lima, this scene is typical and is played out in multiple locations for two weeks of COP meetings each year. While in 2009 Copenhagen provided free public-transport cards for COP participants as it had commensurate adequate public transportation options, a practice that was repeated in France during the 2015 COP21 Paris negotiations, the bus I'm on now could just as easily have been one that transported me to meetings in Cancun in 2010 or Doha in 2012. Truly, only the scenery outside the window varies. The specifics of the discussions change from year to year, yet there are continuities in substance and jargon. I hear someone say, 'This one reads "market mechanisms" ...'. Someone else says, '... and market mechanisms in the new agreement ...'. I hear phrases peppered with acronyms such as 'climate and the SDGs'. I know that they are referring to the sustainable development goals. I can't really catch the conversations in any coherent sense. The owner of the backpack that has occupied the seat next to me migrates up towards the front of the bus and confers with another participant then heads back to his original group saying something about 'integrated climate risk management for resilient ... [inaudible] ... under the agenda item involving "Trade and Climate Change: Exploring a New Agenda".' Now two people are swaying in the aisle having abandoned their seats to discuss something related to 'international insights on China'. One heads back towards the front of the bus to confer with a colleague then reports back in German. I hear the English phrase 'enabling conditions at sub-national level'. He checks a text message. And another. He says something about Malaysia. He's reading something off his phone while his colleagues lean in to better hear what he is saying. Another man pulls something out of his bag—a bag that clearly came from another climate-related meeting based on the logo emblazoned on the front. He checks some notes he made on the slightly rumpled document in his hand, refers to his phone, and then continues to engage in the ongoing conversation.

Even as the bus arrives at the meeting venue, participants continue to talk shop as they shuffle off the bus and follow the designated way into the first building of the conference venue, where we are all instructed towards specific lines that will take us through security which is strikingly similar to the security we went through in various airports as we flew to Lima to attend these meetings. We are allowed to keep our shoes on (perhaps it is undignified for delegates to remove their shoes), but laptops and liquids come out into bins, and we are asked to walk through metal detectors. UN security members beckon us through the lines and herd us towards the entrance to the next section of the building, where our lanyard badges with barcodes are scanned as we enter the sprawling area containing the buildings where negotiations are held. Those scanning our badges glance at their computer screens to see that the photo that comes up indeed matches with the wearer of the badge, smile, and say, 'Have a good day' or 'Good luck'—seemingly knowing that what lies ahead of us is not an easy task. I was struck by this more recently in Paris, where, at the Métro stop for Le Bourget, where the meetings were being held, people in COP21 vests ushered us towards shuttles that would take us out to the meeting spaces. 'Bonne chance!', said the surprisingly cheerful workers, pointing us towards the lines forming for the shuttles and onto buses emblazoned with infor-mation in French regarding their fuel-saving characteristics, which include training drivers in fuel-saving driving techniques. Where do these people work when they aren't employed in vast numbers to facili-tate the very basic yet crucial work of getting negotiators to the loca-tion of the deliberations? How is it that they recognise that 'luck' is what is needed, as the agreements often seem poised to fail until well beyond the designated closing time for each meeting? What must they see as thousands of people migrate by them daily—some carrying briefcases and dressed as 'professional' delegates and others wearing more 'activist' attire, decrying the injustices of REDD+ programmes or policies, demanding that the World Bank stay out of climate-change funding, or that fossil fuels be kept in the ground?

Most of us are clearly comfortable in this world, regardless of whether we have been here before. Most of us *have* been here before, but far away from the literal geographical 'here'—we've been ushered to shuttles and wished luck in multiple languages and by people of varying nationalities. In many ways, from an ethnographic standpoint, this is what makes the UN negotiations a 'site' worthy of exploration. Its norms, rules, and procedures are replicated in a variety of different geo-graphical locations, yet, while each iteration is distinctive in particular ways, each also contains familiar components that circumscribe what it means to do policy work within the context of UN negotiations.

Throughout my participation in UN meetings, contrary to the impression the preceding description may have given, my goal has not been to eavesdrop on the conversations of delegates but to observe and document how it is that the work of policy-making is actually done in the particular locations within which policy is negotiated. In the spirit of ethnography, I have been attentive to the specifics surrounding what it means to be a seasoned participant in UN negotiations. Clearly, the UN represents a work context within which identifiable individuals apply their work knowledges in order to engage effectively in the making of policy. Rather than being an abstract and obscure process, as Courtney Smith explores in her *Politics and Processes at the United Nations: The Global Dance* (2006), the workings of the UN are as choreographed by bureaucratic particularities and specific norms as other work environments with which we might be more familiar. Smith describes this as follows:

> At any particular UN gathering, there are member-state delegates, Secretariat officials, and NGO representatives, each of whom may begin in his or her own little group or clique. Some of the members of the dance troupe naturally assume a role at the center of the dance floor; these lead dancers include the most powerful member states of the organization and those members who are most directly affected by the issue at hand. Gathered around these lead dancers would be a variety of supporting players: middle power states that serve as brokers, bringing together different key attendees to see if they can dance in the same routine; members of the organization's staff, who serve as the orchestra, offering music and language that have fostered common movements in the past; representatives of civil society who seek to get the lead dancers and other players to consider new moves and music that has not been used before; and otherwise marginalized members, who lurk as outcasts around the perimeter, able to influence the unfolding dance only by attempting to block or disrupt it.
>
> (Smith 2006: 4–5)

In moving between ethnographic description of these work contexts and elaborations on specific policy 'moments' as certain policies were negotiated, my aim is to contribute in a concrete way to discussions surrounding the implications of recent transformations in global environmental governance.

Background: The UN in context

Founded as an intergovernmental institution to help ensure peace following World War II, the UN has become one of the most iconic institutions of global governance. 'The work of the UN reaches every corner of the globe', pronounces the 'UN at a Glance' segment of the UN website (UN, n.d.). In fact, a Google search of the preceding quoted phrase indicates that it has been taken up verbatim in a wide variety of web-based settings, from the UK-specific UN informational website, to a page devoted to proclaiming 'Happy United Nations Day' in the context of a site related the 'United Nations Social Development Network' which appears to be a digest of news related to UN-based activities of interest to individuals who work in areas related to international development. The simultaneous existence of this exact phrase in a variety of disparate locations is somewhat metaphorical for the UN itself. While the specifics of work being addressed by individuals who engage in making policy under the auspices of the UN varies, there are clear mandates, work processes, and bureaucratic linkages between various institutions through which UN work is accomplished.

As the quintessential behemoth bureaucracy, the UN is simultaneously well known and obscure. Although the far-reaching global nature of the UN can lend to greater visibility of its presence, the sheer scope of programmes and institutions that fall under the auspices of the UN concurrently contributes to a lack of general understanding about the *actual* work that gets done under its auspices. To most of us, the most visible representations of the UN are related to blue helmets, Security Council decisions, or newsworthy statements made by the secretary general. These references are fragmented and disconnected from the processes within which they are engendered. What goes on inside the meetings, hallways, and offices of various UN buildings around the world is not readily accessible to most individuals, in part due to limited access to UN activities and in part due to the sheer scope and complexity of UN work.

On a basic level, the UN is a high-profile entity that conducts varied and far-reaching work through its six main bodies: (1) the General Assembly, (2) the Security Council, (3) the ECOSOC, (4) the Trusteeship Council, (5) the International Court of Justice, and (6) the Secretariat. Extending far beyond these actual identifiable bodies of the institution are the offices and organisations that comprise elements of the UN bureaucracy around the world. While all of these varied elements make speaking of the UN as a single entity challenging at best, here in this book I narrow the view to focus on the work that gets done within the context of actual negotiations primarily related to the specific deliberating bodies I identified in Chapter 1: the UNFCCC, the CBD, the UNFF, and the UNPFII.

As will become clear throughout this analysis, the work taking place in these arenas is likewise obscure as a result of the fact that environmental agreements (and those involving Indigenous Peoples) tap into wide-ranging legal, scientific, social, political, and economic arenas—often in fairly unpredictable or unanticipated ways. Given the situated character of ethnographic research along with the relative lack of common knowledge of the actual logistics of deliberating policy under the UN, this chapter is designed to fill in key details so that readers can gain a more comprehensive sense of the specific cases and examples provided in subsequent chapters. What it means to 'make policy' within the context of an entity such as the UN merits some background explanation. How are governments and other participants invested in particular language or text? The analysis in the chapters that follow address these issues as they pertain to particular cases.

Inside the bureaucracy

To the external observer, simply viewing actual negotiations would not lend a great degree of clarity as to how things work, as one sees participants milling about Plenary and 'Working Group' meetings, delegates making 'interventions' when called on by the Chair, and discussions going on in more informal locations such as cafeterias, delegate lounges, and even transportation to meetings, such as the circumstance I described at the start of this chapter. Infused with diplomatic phrases, jargon, acronyms, and policy-specific language, the significance of the content of interventions made by participants in policy negotiations is difficult to interpret by all but the seasoned participant. My early experiences attending UN meetings at the Palais des Nations in Geneva in the late 1990s speak to the specifics of work in UN meetings—specifics that often need to be learned through experience. The neophyte participant, as I very much was upon entering the UN headquarters in Geneva to attend the meetings of the Intergovernmental Forum on Forests (IFF), soon learns that, until the terrain becomes familiar, there are challenges associated with locating documents, learning which participants are allowed to attend or engage in specific meetings, figuring out just where to sit and how to access informal discussions associated with different agenda items. These are daunting lessons to learn, as any ethnographer is loath to make obvious mistakes and gaffes.

In the realm of international policy, though, these are the easy parts to learn, as a careful observer can develop a working knowledge of how to 'be' in the setting. Added to this learning curve is the learning associated with the given policy terrain being negotiated.

Within the context of the deliberations, a highly routinised and diplomatic process unfolds as participants take up various issues related to the meetings at hand. These issues have an extensive history and a highly complex language associated with them. For example, the following statement ('intervention') made during the Fourth Comité de Paris meeting on the evening of 9 December 2015, makes little sense out of context:

> Mr. President, the Cook Islands aligns itself to the statements made by G77 and AOSIS. The Cook Islands believe that limiting the global temperature change to below 1.5 degrees Celsius is critical for the survival of our islands and their people. Loss and Damage must be a separate and distinct Article in the new agreement. On the finance Article, it is an improvement. However, more work is needed in this regard. We are concerned there is no reference to SIDS and LDCs. SIDS and LDCs must be fully recognized. For us this is about access and simplifying the procedures for existing resources—not vulnerability.
>
> (Field notes, 9 December 2015)

Clearly, a strong working knowledge of the negotiations is necessary to understand this intervention by the Cook Islands. Even if one were to become familiar with the role of the Alliance Of Small Island States (AOSIS) in the negotiations (Ashe et al. 1999; Betzold, 2010; Betzold et al. 2012) and how it is that alliances between member-states with common interests work in UN negotiations (Bressler 2004; Chatterjee and Finger 1994; Smith 2006), or even the history of the negotiations surrounding 'Loss and Damage' (Stabinsky and Hoffmaister 2015), understanding the substance of the Cook Islands' intervention requires not only an immersion in the issues being taken up by the larger climate regime but also close attention to the negotiations as they transform over the course of the particular meeting. Here, the Cook Islands' intervention references the (then) current iteration of the negotiating text. The reference to the improvement to the 'finance Article' is highly significant, as the issue of 'finance'—and what that has come to mean in climate negotiations—was extremely contentious at COP21 in Paris. Virtually every delegate and non-governmental participant in the room at the time of this intervention knew the significance of this element of the Cook Islands' intervention—and it was certainly expected that it would be noted by the president of the COP as signalling a lack of consensus on the text.

Digging through drudgery for data

While Courtney Smith (2006), quoted above, likens the coordinated actions of participants during deliberations to a dance, her description implies a certain level of action and excitement that is rarely representative of UN negotiations. In fact, those of us who research UN meetings often jest about the tedious nature of the deliberations. Hours are spent hashing over small bits of text, and statements by governments are veiled in diplomatic representations of their interests. Yet researchers to whom I have spoken agree that there is something fascinating about the dynamics that unfold throughout the processes of negotiation. Smith's (2006) characterisation of the participants' roles in the process speaks to these larger dynamics that become visible: from the norms of diplomacy, to the strategic moves that participants make in order to attempt to influence the various outcomes, to the variety of roles that individuals play in the processes and unequal power arrangements associated with how people and delegations are positioned in the processes. These are roles that are contingent on how individuals are located in (or gain access to) the negotiations, but they are also related to the specific dynamics that emerge during particular deliberations. Through the case-study elaborations on particular negotiations that I use in this book, I give particular examples of how members of civil society, in Smith's terms, 'seek to get the lead dancers and other players to consider new moves and music that has not been used before' (2006: 5). While Smith is speaking metaphorically, the dynamics whereby participants in multilateral global governance aim to influence policy processes are addressed in the substantive chapters of this book as I move analytically between concrete examples of policy negotiations and the larger implications of transitions in policy debates.

Additionally, it is imperative to contextualise the negotiations, as the Cook Islands' intervention quoted above was intended to illustrate. This contextualisation includes not only the specifics of the negotiations as they evolve over the span of particular meetings but also the broader scope of norms, rules, and expectations that serve to organise global governance. Reus-Smit points out the fundamental premise that 'states negotiate environmental accords within a pre-existing complex of social institutions' (1996: 103). This seems fairly obvious, but much of my learning process regarding the workings of actual negotiations has been to gain an understanding of just what those 'social institutions' are. While international relations theorists might be more willing to identify norms associated with 'realism' or other dynamics associated with the theoretical frameworks debated in international relations, as a sociologist and an ethnographer, I take seriously the premise that the social institutions that organise negotiations span both the micro (interpersonal norms of interaction) to the macro (perceived exigencies of a current globalised economic system, for example) and all sorts of coordinated levels in between. Powerful nation-states steer negotiations in particular ways, while members of the Secretariat or Co-Chairs of meetings prepare the texts upon which the deliberations are based. The 'power' of nation-states is based not solely on their positioning in a global economy but also to a large degree on other factors such as their immediate relevance to the negotiations (e.g., Brazil's vast tropical forests) or their relative disproportionate experiences of environmental degradation, such as the aforementioned AOSIS in the climate negotiations (Betzold et al. 2012). Blocks of countries, such as AOSIS or the G77 (originally the 'Group of 77' developing countries, now signifying the block of all developing countries), strategise about how to influence the 'language' of the texts, as members of civil society and Indigenous Peoples lobby government delegates to include certain language in their interventions or, when permitted, make statements on their own behalf. However, the context within which these factors are enacted is significant. To say that governments form alliances in order to leverage more power in negotiations does not address the complexities of *how* this strategy works in negotiations. The following chapters will take up these dynamics (and others) in detail as I explore specific issues that I take as 'cases'.

As I mentioned in Chapter 1, my choice of cases to use for analysis was guided by civil society and Indigenous Peoples who participated in the various processes I observed. Each of the cases emerged as being worthy of attention to non-governmental participants. However, prior to developing the specific analysis associated with these cases in the following chapters, it is important to establish the foundation of *how* UN-based environmental negotiations work in practice, so that readers who are unfamiliar with this work setting can get a sense of how it is that documents such as the ones represented in Figures 2.1 and 2.2 are actually produced.

The UN as a research site

In ethnographic research, setting the scene is a crucial part of the study, as space organises individuals' activities in significant ways. Additionally, the organisation of space often reflects particular institutional exigencies, goals, and norms. Smith, referenced earlier, has characterised the players in the deliberations—from the Secretariat,

NON-PAPER
1:1pm, 26.5 October 2010

[TITLE TO READ: Agriculture and biodiversity: Consideration of ways and
means to promote the positive and minimize the negative impacts of the
production and use of biofuels on biodiversity];

The Conference of the Parties,

Recalling decision IX/2 of the Conference of the Parties;

PREAMBLE

[Recognizing that the recommendations of the decisions on
agricultural biodiversity, also apply to the production of biofuels feedstocks
to biofuels;]

[Recognizing that continuing scientific uncertainty and concern exists
in regard to given the scientific uncertainty that exists, and the recent
information that has emerged, significant concern surrounds the potential
intended and unintended impacts of biofuels on biodiversity [and impacts on
biodiversity, that would affect socio-economic conditions and food and
energy security resulting from the production and use of biofuels [as well as
impacts on [land security][land-tenure security where they are relevant for
the implementation of the CBD] and on indigenous and local communities;]

[Also rRecognizing that, improved research, monitoring and
evaluation, scientific, socio-economic, and sustainability scientific and
environmental assessments, open and transparent consultation, with the full
and effective participation of indigenous and local communities, and
information flow are crucial needs for the continuing improvement of policy
guidance, and decision making, in order to address the uncertainties and
concerns that exist regarding the potential intended and unintended impacts
of biofuels on biodiversity and impacts on biodiversity that would affect
related socio-economic conditions and to promote the positive and minimize
or avoid the negative impacts of biofuels on biodiversity and the impacts on

Figure 2.1 CBD COP10 'Non-Paper' on 'biofuels and biodiversity' (p. 1).
Reprinted with permission of the United Nations.

to government negotiators, to civil society participants. Given the centrality of these actors in my research, I'll elaborate further on their roles
and activities later as I tie their actions into the specific cases I develop
and analyse in subsequent chapters. However, the actual context of
these deliberations and discussions merits some attention, as I have
noted that the UN is not a site that is familiar to most individuals, with
the exception of those who participate in the processes of negotiation or
who cover those negotiations as members of the press. Anyone who has
taken a tour of the UN headquarters in New York City, for example,
has gained a sense that work is being carried out within the meeting
rooms, offices, halls, and cafeterias through which they are guided.
Glimpsing news coverage of General Assembly or other UN Plenary
meetings can also provide some insights into how things are 'set up'

UNEP

 CBD

**Convention on
Biological Diversity**

Distr.
GENERAL

UNEP/CBD/COP/DEC/X/37
29 October 2010

ORIGINAL: ENGLISH

CONFERENCE OF THE PARTIES TO THE
CONVENTION ON BIOLOGICAL DIVERSITY
Tenth meeting
Nagoya, Japan, 18-29 October 2010
Agenda item 6.4

**DECISION ADOPTED BY THE CONFERENCE OF THE PARTIES TO THE CONVENTION
ON BIOLOGICAL DIVERSITY AT ITS TENTH MEETING**

X/37. Biofuels and biodiversity

The Conference of the Parties,

Recalling its decision IX/2, in which it decided to consider at its tenth meeting ways and means to promote the positive and minimize the negative impacts of the production and use of biofuels on biodiversity,

Recognizing that improved scientific, environmental and socio-economic research and assessments, open and transparent consultation, with the full and effective participation of the concerned indigenous and local communities, and sharing of best practices, are crucial needs for the continuing improvement of policy guidance and decision-making to promote the positive and minimize or avoid the negative impacts of biofuels on biodiversity and impacts on biodiversity that affect related socioeconomic conditions and to address the gaps in scientific knowledge and concerns that exist regarding such impacts,

Noting the rapid pace of development of new technologies that enable conversion of biomass into a broader and more flexible range of fuels,

Acknowledging concerns that deployment of biofuel technologies, may result in increased demand for biomass and aggravate drivers of biodiversity loss, such as land use change, introduction of invasive alien species, bearing in mind paragraph 6 of decision X/38 of the Conference of the Parties, and resource over-consumption,

Also acknowledging the potential for biofuel technologies to make a positive contribution to mitigating climate change, another of the main drivers of biodiversity loss, and generating additional income in rural areas,

Aware in particular of the potential positive and negative impacts of the production and use of biofuels on the conservation and customary use of biodiversity by indigenous and local communities, and the consequences for their well-being,

1.   *Expresses its gratitude* to the European Union for its financial contribution towards the regional workshops for Latin America and the Caribbean, and Asia and the Pacific, and to the Government of Germany for the regional workshop for Africa and to the Governments of Brazil, Thailand and Ghana for hosting these workshops to facilitate active participation of the entire region;

/...

Figure 2.2 CBD COP10 Decision X/37 (p. 1). Reprinted with permission of the United Nations.

at the UN. Participants with ear pieces used for translation, situated around concentric circles of desks—their placards clearly displaying their institutionally-recognised identity—these are images with which we are familiar. However, this limited view into the workings of the UN is most likely disconnected from the less visible work and sequences of actions that typify UN deliberations—some of which I have described in 'ethnographic snippets' in this and the previous chapter.

The iconic Plenary hall is, indeed, a significant location for UN policy negotiations in terms of representing one of the spaces where deliberations of policy unfold. Flanked by glassed-in interpretation booths where all formal statements are translated into the six official UN languages, country delegations are typically located in rows or concentric semicircles of tables that face the raised location of the Meeting Chair (or Co-Chairs) and members of the Secretariat. From this vantage point, Chairs and Co-Chairs can identify country delegations that have signalled their interest in making an intervention. But the Plenary hall is just one location of many where policy work is accomplished. In fact, much of the work is completed in the compiling of texts prior to the actual negotiations and, subsequently, in the smaller Working Groups and informal negotiations that take place in the corridors, cafeterias, and other spaces that may not be specifically designated as work spaces yet are used by negotiators during the span of meetings.

Meetings: Location, duration, and procedure

Much UN work extends far beyond the scope of my research, as the locations of actual policy deliberations exist as my primary research sites. As I am focusing on the deliberations of particular aspects of policy, I likewise focus on the sites where those deliberations have primarily taken place. This includes UN headquarters and conference centres that have been reserved for the purposes of UN meetings. However, each of the above-mentioned bodies has its own schedule of meetings. In the case of the UNFCCC, COPs take place for a two-week period every year (typically from late November to mid December). These are held in different locations around the world, often in sprawling convention centres where larger Plenary rooms and smaller Working-Group rooms can be accommodated. As I discussed in Chapter 1, governments offer to host COPs and are then tasked with ensuring that the appropriate infrastructure is in place by the time the meetings are held. The CBD works similarly, except that COPs currently take place every 2 years. Given that the UNFF is not associated with a legally binding agreement, it has no 'Parties' and therefore no COPs. However, the main meetings ('sessions') of the UNFF take place approximately every year and extend for either a week or a two-week period. With the exception of UNFF3 and UNFF4 (in 2004 and 2005), which took place in Geneva, and UNFF10 (which was held in Istanbul, Turkey, in 2013), to date UNFF meetings have been held at UN Headquarters in New York City. The UNPFII typically meets in the spring every year at UN headquarters in New York City for a two-week period. 'Ad-hoc expert group' (AHEG) or simply 'expert group' meetings related to various agenda items are held for shorter periods of time in various locations ranging from New York to Vienna to Nairobi. Scheduled 'intersessional' meetings of these bodies likewise take place in a variety of locations around the globe, typically lasting from one to two weeks. For example, 'Working-Group' meetings associated with the CBD are typically scheduled for one week and meet either once or twice per year, depending upon the agenda items that are being addressed.

Meetings themselves are extremely intense, especially for government delegations and particularly-invested CSOs and IPOs, who meet fairly constantly outside of officially scheduled meetings, often late into the night and early in the morning. This is especially true during the second week of negotiations at COPs, when host countries are eager to finalise agreements and avoid deliberative failures. Participants who are interested in maintaining their engagement with the deliberations need to be available at all hours to access documents as they are revised and disseminated. Delegations then meet to assess new 'language' in the texts for how it reflects their negotiating position, and plan how to respond to the revisions if the substance of their interventions has not been incorporated. Non-governmental participants strategise as to how to influence the process, as governments' positions become clearer and coalitions around divisive elements are formed.

UN meetings are notorious for starting late. It is not unusual for a Plenary session that is scheduled to start at 10.00 a.m. to actually begin closer to 11.00, particularly as the meetings progress and delegates are pulled in a variety of directions, as concurrent Working Groups are deliberating specific agenda items, and as delegations need to hash out how it is they will address particular problem areas of the negotiating texts. This tension is often raised by governments with small delegations, as they feel as though they need to be in multiple places at once in order to keep up with the most recent changes and discussions surrounding each agenda item. Negotiations are equally notorious for *going* late—often well past the final designated time in the evening (contingent, in some cases, on the availability of translators who, unlike negotiators, often have stipulations on how long they are allowed to work). Additionally, while UNFCCC COPs are scheduled to end on the Friday of the second week, participants understand that it is more typical for deliberations to extend well into Saturday. It is not uncommon for negotiations to appear to be in complete disarray until drastic moves are taken by Chairs to encourage agreement on difficult segments of the texts. This often happens well beyond the original designated time of completion for the meetings. This is particularly true when there is an especially important agenda item being addressed. Host countries put pressure on participants to come to a consensus so that the meeting can be deemed a success. For example, at the UNFCCC's COP21 in Paris in 2015, the French presidency of the COP was extremely influential in facilitating agreements among various governments who were finding great difficulty coming to consensus on elements of the negotiating texts. Participants regularly remarked that the French presidency was not going to allow Paris to be a failure. Indeed, the Danish presidency of COP15 in Copenhagen was critiqued for creating many of the issues that served to contribute to the ultimately highly disappointing outcome of the negotiations. Host governments and meeting Chairs go to great lengths to ensure that consensus can be reached.

Rules of procedure are typically consistent across the major meetings of the various bodies but vary according to the type of meeting (COP versus AHEG, for example). Conventional practices, such as nongovernmental access to 'closed' (to all but government delegates) meetings, tend to be consistent in theory but somewhat flexible in practice. Chairs may decide to enforce the 'closed' nature of specific meetings depending upon the level of contention among government delegates, or in cases where governments voice concerns about nongovernmental access. Meetings of designated groups, such as the G77 and China, or the European Union are, except in very specific circumstances, closed to non-members of that group. It is understood that governments will not attend meetings of the environmental NGOs (ENGOs) at UNFCCC meetings, with the exception of individuals who have a history of working with ENGOs yet who may be serving on government delegations for a particular meeting. It is not unheard of for governments to give credentials to individuals who work for environmental organisations, either to gain from their perspective or simply to allow them to have access to meetings. However, governments vary widely on their stances related to the participation of non-governmental actors in UN policy processes—in fact, as Chapter 3 will explore in greater detail, the politics of participation are regularly debated in UN meetings. Therefore, not all governments credential participants who also have allegiances to other groups of participants—doing so can be seen as taking a political stance on practices that promote transparency and participation for members of civil society.

Texts: the UN documentary reality

Not only does one need to be an experienced practitioner to picture the actual activities that are typically involved in generating and negotiating texts through the UN, but, as Figures 2.1 and 2.2 clearly illustrate, one must be an experienced participant to understand the meaning behind the debates over language that typify UN negotiations. Texts are central to the negotiating process, yet their content is the subject of intense and protracted debates—debates that become invisible in the final documentation, as is represented in the difference between the two documents represented in Figures 2.1 and 2.2. Not only does a 'final' text explicitly point to a legacy of other events and negotiated documents by referencing past agreements, but it also contains the residue of multiple often highly contentious debates, such as the ones that the CBD Secretariat attempted to capture in the mark-up to the document represented in Figure 2.1. Analysis of text and documents in UN negotiations can be seen as a multilayered enterprise. It is typically quite possible to map out the documentary complex of a particular negotiating process by following the explicit textual legacy of documents referenced in the final text. It is important to note that there were multiple iterations of the document that ultimately became the one represented in Figure 2.2. Each successive meeting of a particular Working Group results in a new draft of a document which is intended to capture the main points of the debate yet also move closer to consensus. There is often protracted debate about whether a particular delegation's position has been captured in the next iteration of the document, yet the Chairs are in the position of having to construct a document that contains consensus text in order to reach agreement and therefore must make decisions about which elements of the negotiations are included in the next document.

Often, drafts of negotiating texts are made available to participants prior to the actual negotiations. These often take the form of a 'Chair's text' which provide a basis for negotiations. These texts can then be traced through to the 'final' documents, which are 'adopted' by the participants of the given meeting. For example, COP12 of the CBD held in 2014 produced 100 official documents and thirty-five 'decisions'. However, this sort of documentary tracing would provide a relatively uninteresting picture of actual negotiations, as the strategic nature and actualities of negotiation would be lost in such an exercise. For example, even with the mark-up that is apparent in Figure 2.1, two important elements are unclear. The first element that is invisible is *who* provided the substance for the comment on the text. The second piece that is not recorded in the document is *why* that particular text change was important to the nation who intervened. As it was a text from a Working Group, we know that the text-change requests were made by nation-states, as non-governmental participants are not allowed to engage in those deliberations except by lobbying government delegates. Being present in the room is the only way to know the answer to the first element that is missing—and speaking with other delegates or knowing the history of particular positions on language is the only way to understand the second missing piece.

Going deeper into the process, one can speak to those involved with the negotiations to try to recreate the history of why particular phrases become so contentious whereas others make it into the final text without further discussion. Observing negotiations helps to fill in this particular level in terms of identifying political interests of participants in advocating for (or against) specific terminology.

Finally, the most invisible layer, yet one of the most important, involves the larger discursive frameworks that organise the negotiations themselves, such as the influence of discourses of neoliberal economic imperatives on the process of negotiation and the organising capabilities of concepts such as 'market mechanisms' or 'impediments to trade'. Asking questions about the impact of these larger discursive frames typically befuddles delegates as they are tasked to ensure that they make interventions that are consistent with their national position on a particular agenda item. The immediate work of negotiating texts requires that delegates clearly understand their governments' views on particular agenda items and terminology. A strong negotiator is not one who goes off script. As a sociologist analysing this particular phenomenon, my role is to assess all of these various levels. This requires being attentive to the actual discussions surrounding the text *and* to anchor those debates within the context of the larger social relations that circumscribe negotiations.

MEAs: History, context, and critique

The primary policy processes on which I focus (UNFCCC, CBD) had their official origins in the 1992 United Nations Conference on Environment and Development (UNCED). The same is true for the UNFF. Thus, the UNCED agenda along with the shifting politics of engagement of NGOs in the UN shaped the goals and objectives of the agreements in important ways. Otherwise known as the 'Earth Summit',

UNCED represented a key turning point in intergovernmental environmental policy. Preceded by the 1972 Stockholm Conference on the Human Environment, UNCED raised environmental issues to a new level of international prominence by resulting in three legally-binding agreements (on climate, biological diversity, and desertification), a non-legally binding 'statement' on forests, which ultimately paved the way for the UNFF, and 'Agenda 21'—a blueprint for addressing environmental issues into the twenty-first century. The legally-binding agreements that came out of UNCED are just three of many MEAs that have been negotiated in similar fashion.

Not only did UNCED create a policy basis for future negotiations through the agreements that governments negotiated and, in some cases, ratified, but it also established a precedent for the participation of civil society in UN environmental policy. By the time of UNCED, about 1,400 NGOs had registered with the UNCED Secretariat as accredited participants. However, UNCED was also marked by extreme criticism about the *substance* of civil society contributions to the actual process. Chatterjee and Finger, for example, based on their involvement with the pre-UNCED and UNCED negotiations, argued that, while members of civil society were increasingly being incorporated into UN deliberations, their concerns were not finding their way into the *results* of those deliberations (Chatterjee and Finger 1994). Significantly, critics of UNCED and its resulting MEAs have questioned the capacity for negotiations under the UN to create real social or environmental change. Those who have analysed the effectiveness of the UN as a forum for environmental negotiations (see, for example, Chatterjee and Finger 1994; Elliot 1998; Mische and Ribeiro 1998), have questioned its ability to affect environmental change due in part to the fragmented nature of the UN system but also to the primacy of the principle of nation-state sovereignty within the UN system. Clearly, the very purpose of the UN creates the context within which negotiations are designed to reflect governments' interests. My decision to focus on the dynamics that became important to CSOs and IPOs allowed for a focus on the critiques of what it was that governments bring to the table—namely highly politicised positions that were often disconnected from the environmental problems that the meetings purported to address.

What is a 'normal' intervention?

My previous discussions of 'diplomatic language' merely scratch the surface of what it is that delegates *do* as they make 'interventions'. It is important for readers to understand that delegates rarely speak without script—in line with Smith's description of the choreographed nature of negotiations referenced earlier, gaining a sense of how negotiations work includes understanding the fact that the majority of interventions are highly scripted statements. I have participated in the drafting of these scripted statements, yet only within the context of interventions made by non-governmental participants. It is not unusual for NGOs, at their morning meetings during which they discuss the current status of texts and governments' positions on particular issues, to establish a 'drafting' group. This group would be composed of individuals who are willing to begin work on writing a statement that a particular group of NGOs would deliver in reference to a specific agenda item, should time permit after interventions made by governments during plenaries and working-group sessions. I understand the process of drafting these statements to be quite similar among delegations, ranging from Indigenous Peoples' groups to government delegations. Within this context, there is a close attention to the language of the current text and what it is that the participant (or group of participants) would like to see included in the final document. In order to illustrate this process and to give readers a sense of how negotiations unfold, I will include some segments of actual interventions in the context of an 'ethnographic snippet' and then briefly analyse and explain them.

'Ethnographic snippet': CBD SBSTTA22

It is 2018, and I'm now in Montreal. I'm here to attend the twenty-second meeting of the Subsidiary Body on Scientific, Technical, and Technological Advice (SBSTTA) of the CBD. It is early July, but North America is experiencing a heatwave, so my entrance into the air-conditioned International Civil Aviation Organization (ICAO) building provides relief from the heat and humidity. The headquarters of the CBD is located in Montreal, and the ICAO has the appropriate set-up for intergovernmental meetings, from security at the entrance, to small meeting rooms, a 'bistro' that provides coffee and snacks, and a large Plenary hall.

I have already picked up my entry badge, which identifies my credentials—the lower segment of my badge states 'EDUCATION' and has a pink swath along the bottom. Those who have received credentials as NGOs have badges that clearly state 'NGO' and contain a grey swath. Members of Indigenous Peoples and local communities' badges state 'IPLC', associated with a purple swath. Governments that have ratified the Convention are identified as 'PARTY' with a large green stripe at the bottom of the badge—a format that is useful for identifying who is allowed to enter meetings that are open only to government delegates.

I pass the 'bistro' area and note that people are clustered around tables with laptops open, discussing texts and negotiations. I go to the fourth floor and enter the Plenary hall, finding a place to sit near the placard stating 'EDUCATION'. The Plenary hall contains raised seating in the front of the room for meeting Chairs and members of the Secretariat, rows of parallel desks with microphones and ear pieces for governments and other participants, and booths for simultaneous translation in the back. Chairs and members of the Secretariat and a rapporteur sit facing all other participants in front of a large emblem of the ICAO, flanked by flags of this same emblem.

This morning, participants are slated to address Agenda Item 9: 'Biodiversity and Climate Change: Ecosystem-Based Approaches to Climate Change Adaptation and Disaster Risk Reduction'. At 10.15, the meeting begins, with a member of the CBD Secretariat inviting the participants 'to consider the draft recommendations provided in this document', referring to the document associated with Item 9 of the agenda. The representative of the Secretariat concludes her comments and thanks the Chair. At that point, the Chair states, 'Thank you Secretariat. I will now open the floor for interventions on Item 9.' There is a pause as various government delegations press the button in front of them indicating a desire to speak. 'Well, we have a growing list of speakers', notes the Chair. He goes on:

Ah, before we begin the interventions I would like to ask everyone taking the floor to respect the time limit of three minutes so we can allow as many as possible to speak. Please be concise, constructive, and to the point. And then hand in your statement to the Secretariat to be registered. But please do not substitute time with speed. Speak slowly for the interpreters so that everyone can hear what you are saying. Now I would like to give the floor to Mexico. Mexico, you have the floor.

In this prelude to allowing governments to make their interventions, the Chair has stated several points related to actual negotiations. First, he notes that there is 'a growing list of speakers'. It is typical for most governments who are engaged in the agenda item to give a preliminary intervention related to that agenda item. He further notes that there is a limited amount of time. Over the course of a given meeting, agenda items are slated to be discussed during specific time frames. However, the more contentious issues tend to garner more interventions from many governments, with several governments asking to take the floor more than once. This can cause the agenda item to take more than its allotted time, eating into the time period that was previously designated for another item. When this happens, the Chair typically decides to establish a 'contact group' which is designed to provide a forum for delegates to hash out their disagreements. Contact-group meetings tend to be closed to non-governmental participants (hence the utility of a clear 'Party' identification badge), yet this is at the discretion of the Chair. Lastly, the Chair, in his statement made prior to opening the floor, acknowledges the fact that simultaneous translation is taking place. While English is the dominant language of negotiations, many participants require translation. This can present problems, as meanings of specific terms are not necessarily known by interpreters. When this sort of confusion arises, non-English speaking delegations may take the floor in order to ask for a clarification.

After the Chair opens the floor and calls on Mexico to make the first intervention, Mexico's negotiator speaks for approximately a minute and a half, which is noted as being 'short' by the appreciative Chair. Thanking Mexico, the Chair then calls upon Norway. I quote Norway's intervention below in its entirety, as it contained multiple elements that typify both diplomatic language and substantive contributions of most interventions:

> Thank you, Chair. Norway welcomes continued work with climate change under the CBD and would like to see continued close cooperation with the Climate Convention, the UNFCCC. Although the Climate Convention is the main body for addressing climate-change issues, the CBD plays an important role in highlighting the importance of ecosystems and the protection of biodiversity in climate mitigation and adaptation. Suggestions for how to integrate ecosystem services into approaches to climate change adaptation and disaster-risk reduction are well placed within CBD's scope of expertise. Norway is pleased to see this brought forward at SBSTTA and welcomes the voluntary draft guidelines presented under this agenda item. In Cancun, the Parties of the CBD agreed to encourage Parties to take into account the importance of insuring the integrity of all ecosystems and the protection of biodiversity when developing their Nationally Determined Contributions— their NDCs—to the Climate Convention and the Paris Agreement. In December, a few days after the CBD COP in Egypt, the Parties of the Climate Convention will convene a dialogue to take stock of the collective efforts towards the voluntary goals of the Paris

Agreement. This will inform the preparation of the *next* round of updated NDCs to the Paris Agreement. Norway would like to include text along the same lines of the Cancun decision, encouraging Parties to take into account ecosystems and the protection of biodiversity when updating their NDCs. The invitation from the CBD COP will be timely, feeding into the ongoing discussion at the Climate COP that will convene in December. It is clearly stated in the background paper that climate change is predicted to grow as a driver of biodiversity loss, *and* that ecosystems play a key role in climate change mitigation and adaptation. We would therefore like to see the biodiversity climate nexus addressed in preparation for the post-2020 biodiversity framework. We will submit the suggestions to the Secretariat. Thank you very much.

Norway's intervention typifies multiple elements of the negotiating process. First, Norway begins diplomatically. It is not unusual for governments to spend some of their precious seconds thanking the Chair and expressing a commitment to work constructively to come to an agreement on the particular agenda item. In this case, Norway makes a fairly broad statement about the relevance of the CBD to climate negotiations but explicitly asks for the final text on this agenda item to pave the way for an 'invitation' from the next CBD COP to be directed to the Parties of the following UNFCCC COP. The Norwegian delegate has read a carefully scripted statement that is designed not only to emphasise the relevance of biological diversity to climate change but also to suggest particular text be sent on to the next CBD COP in order to contribute to the work of the UNFCCC. Using language that is relevant to the current CBD negotiations ('ecosystem services', 'post-2020 biodiversity framework', for example), and language that is relevant to the climate negotiations (such as 'climate change mitigation and adaptation' and 'NDCs'), Norway's intervention reflects the sort of statement that can be expected in the negotiating arenas I observed.

Interventions continue, with the Chair interjecting at 11.03 to express concern that 'the list of speakers has enlarged' and that time is short. He takes more interventions and then announces at 11.26 that he is 'closing the list of speakers'. As the list of government delegates who wish to make interventions takes the entire time allotted for Agenda Item 9, no CSOs or IPOs make interventions in this session. However, during the afternoon negotiating session, in reference to CBD SBSTTA22 Agenda Item 10, 'Invasive Alien Species', there is time given to 'organisations' after governments have made their statements on the text. Representatives from IPLCs make a statement that includes suggestions to changes to the text. When they have concluded their statement, the Chair of the session states the following: 'I note that IPLCs have suggested language for the text. Do we have support from Parties of this language?' At that point, several governments raise their placards to indicate support. Had no governments indicated support, the text changes referred to in the intervention from the IPLCs would not be included in the next iteration of the negotiating text. Non-governmental participants understand that the substance of their interventions will not be incorporated into the process unless governments also support their positions. Thus, meetings designated for NGOs or IPLCs are important not only for drafting interventions but also for identifying particular sympathetic governments and for creating strategies to lobby them to include particular language in their interventions.

What's in a meeting?

In illustrating the actual work of participants in 'making policy', it is important to explain not only how meetings unfold but also what sorts of issues are on delegates' plates prior to entering the meeting locale. For most meetings, preparatory documents of varying type are available. Agenda items are set prior to meetings, and a 'provisional agenda' is typically one of the first agenda items. A typical agenda for each meeting, at first glance, appears to be overwhelming in its sheer quantity of items and depth of issues. For example, for the SBSTTA22 meeting, the following is a 'list of working documents' and their concomitant agenda-item numbers:

- Revised provisional agenda (CBD/SBSTTA/22/1): Agenda Item 2
- Annotated provisional agenda (CBD/SBSTTA/22/1/Add.1): Agenda Item 2
- Digital sequence information on genetic resources (CBD/SBSTTA/22/2): Agenda Item 3
- Risk assessment and risk management of living modified organisms (CBD/SBSTTA/22/3): Agenda Item 4
- Synthetic biology (CBD/SBSTTA/22/4): Agenda Item 5
- Updated scientific assessment of progress towards selected Aichi Biodiversity Targets and options to accelerate progress (CBD/SBSTTA/22/5): Agenda Item 6
- Overview of relevant information from the regional assessments and the thematic assessment on land degradation by the IPBES, and implications for the work of the Convention (CBD/SBSTTA/22/5/Add.1): Agenda Item 6

- Protected areas and other measures for enhanced conservation and management (CBD/SBSTTA/22/6): Agenda Item 7
- Marine protected areas and spatial planning (CBD/SBSTTA/22/6/Add.1): Agenda Item 7
- Marine and coastal biodiversity (CBD/SBSTTA/22/7): Agenda Item 8
- Summary report on the description of areas meeting the scientific criteria for ecologically or biologically significant marine areas (CBD/SBSTTA/22/7/Add.1): Agenda Item 8
- Ecologically or biologically significant marine areas: options regarding procedures for modification of the descriptions of EBSAs [ecologically or biologically significant areas], describing new areas, and strengthening the scientific process (CBD/SBSTTA/22/7/Add.2): Agenda Item 8
- Biodiversity and climate change: ecosystem-based approaches to climate-change adaptation and disaster risk reduction (CBD/SBSTTA/22/8): Agenda Item 9
- Invasive Alien Species (CBD/SBSTTA/22/9): Agenda Item 10
- Conservation and sustainable use of pollinators (CBD/SBSTTA/22/10): Agenda Item 11
- Second work programme of the IPBES (CBD/SBSTTA/22/11): Agenda Item 12.

Each of these represents a document that is intended to be used as a point of departure in the Plenary sessions. After delegations give 'interventions' on each agenda item, 'conference-room papers', or CRPs, are prepared by the Chairs in consultation with the Secretariat. The goal of the CRPs is to move the discussions closer to 'consensus' by capturing the views of those who have made comments on the documents. These are then turned into 'L' documents, which indicate that the document has 'limited distribution' and has not yet been adopted by the COP. Text that remains contentious is kept in square brackets in order to indicate that it is not 'consensus text'. The often-elusive 'clean text' is one without square brackets, indicating that all governments present during the negotiations agreed to the language encapsulated in the document.

As this chapter has illustrated by way of the use of ethnographic snippets and analysis of actual interventions and agendas, UN deliberations are highly routinised yet also very complex. Participants are required to have very in-depth work knowledges about the most current state of the negotiations. This includes not only understanding the jargon and technical language but also having a sense of what other delegations' positions are. In spite of the fact that there will always be another negotiating session on the horizon, and delegates are often hard-pressed to identify the actual impact of the text they negotiate for 'on-the-ground' realities, deliberations are inevitably protracted and contentious. The following chapters take up these tensions as they manifested themselves in particular issues that emerged during the negotiations over the past decade. While grounded in ethnographic data, the following chapters require a basic sense of the actualities of the negotiating context that this chapter provides.

References

Ashe, J.W., R. Lierop, and A. Cherian (1999) 'The Role of the Alliance of Small Island States (AOSIS) in the Negotiation of the United Nations Framework Convention on Climate Change (UNFCCC)', *Natural Resources Forum*, 23(3): 209–20.

Betzold, C. (2010) ' "Borrowing" Power to Influence International Negotiations: Aosis in the Climate Change Regime, 1990–1997', *Politics*, 30(3): 131–48.

Betzold, C., P. Castro, and F. Weiler (2012) 'AOSIS in the UNFCCC Negotiations: From Unity to Fragmentation?' *Climate Policy*, 12(5): 591–613.

Bressler, M. (2004) *Politics of Trade and Environment and the Transboundary Trade of Genetically Modified Organisms: A Study of Institutional Process, Regime Overlap and North-South Politics in Global Rule-Making*, Berkeley, CA: University of California Press.

Chatterjee, P. and M. Finger (1994) *The Earth Brokers: Power, Politics and World Development*, London and New York: Routledge.

Elliot, L. (1998) 'Greening the United Nations: Future Conditional?' in A. Paolini, A. Jarvis, and C. Reus-Smit (eds.), *Between Sovereignty and Global Governance: The United Nations, the State, and Civil Society*, New York: St. Martin's Press (pp. 135–61).

Mische, P. and M.A. Ribeiro (1998) 'Ecological Security and the United Nations System', in C.F. Alger (ed.), *The Future of the United Nations System: Potential for the Twenty-First Century*, New York: United Nations University Press, pp. 315–56.

Princen, T. and M. Finger (1994) *Environmental NGOs in World Politics: Linking the Local and the Global*, London and New York: Routledge.

Reus-Smit, C. (1996) 'The Normative Structure of International Society', in F. Olser and J. Reppy Hampson (eds), *Earthly Goods: Environmental Change and Social Justice*, Ithaca, NY: Cornell University Press, pp. 96–121.

Smith, Courtney B. (2006) *Politics and Process at the United Nations: The Global Dance*, Boulder, CO: Lynne Rienner Publishers.

Stabinsky, D. and J.P. Hoffmaister (2015) 'Establishing Institutional Arrangements on Loss and Damage under the UNFCCC: The Warsaw International Mechanism for Loss and Damage', *International Journal of Global Warming*, 8(2): 295–318.

UN (n.d.) 'About the UN', available at www.un.org/en/aboutun/index.shtml (accessed 5 January 2015).

—— (n.d.) 'The United Nations at a Glance', available at https://web.archive.org/web/20141225170544/www.un.org/en/aboutun/index.shtml (accessed 5 January 2015).

—— (1993) *Charter of the United Nations and Statute of the International Court of Justice*, New York: UN.

UNEP/UNCED (1992) *The Global Partnership for Environment and Development: A Guide to Agenda 21*, Geneva: UNCED.

3   The contested terrain of action
Civil society in UN climate negotiations

As RINGOS [Research and Independent Non-Governmental Organisations], we take an explicitly non-activist approach. Other NGOs can be political. We can advocate for the science, but we can't take a political position.

(Field notes, 9 December 2015)

Introduction: Raising issues—civil society and climate deliberations

Greeted by a sea of white 'secondary badges' held aloft in symbolic protest for those not so fortunate to have received them, then-Executive Secretary of the UNFCCC, Yvo de Boer, addressed a crowd of civil-society members on 16 December 2009. Seated in the hall outside of the official entrance to the climate-related negotiations at the Bella Center in Copenhagen, Denmark, the civil society representatives did not present de Boer with an easy audience. Throughout the two-week meetings, spanning from 7 to 18 December, tensions surrounding non-governmental access had surfaced in various forms, culminating in severe criticism of the conference organisers when many registered participants were literally left out in the cold as negotiations continued largely among government delegations within the Bella Center.

That conference organisers were overwhelmed by participants surprised many civil society representatives. Growing public concerns about the realities of climate change and the lack of political action on the part of powerful governments created a clear context for civil society interest in the outcome of the Copenhagen deliberations. The ebb and flow of civil society interest in UN climate negotiations is related to the level of importance of items on the agenda. Not only was Copenhagen important for members of civil society due to larger concerns about anthropogenic-caused climate changes, but the importance of COP15 in terms of negotiating a second commitment period for the Kyoto Protocol raised the stakes.

In many ways, the tensions that arose in Copenhagen reflect deeper conflicts within the UN system, particularly as those conflicts pertain to the disconnect between environmental policy-making and 'on-the-ground' realities of environmental degradation. As addressed in previous chapters, the exigencies of governments' political directives often preclude progress towards addressing environmental problems. This intransigence stands in stark contrast to the concerns raised by members of civil society as many CSOs and IPOs bring impassioned evidence of the imperative of immediate action to the negotiations. However, this disjuncture between governments' inaction and civil society activism becomes complex as not all governments eschew activist strategies, and, from time to time, civil society participants form alliances with governments that adopt more activist-related agendas. This chapter addresses this complexity within the context of activism that is designed to push UN-based climate negotiations towards making stronger commitments. Using particular examples from actual negotiations, the chapter argues that 'participation' in environmental policy by members of civil society is not an 'either/or' phenomenon. What it means to participate in policy-making is complex and constantly negotiated, as tensions arise between governments and members of civil society, between civil society and law enforcement in UN-meeting host cities, between governments themselves—and even between members of CSOs. Part of the complexity of these debates involves the meaning and importance attributed to 'access' to the actual meetings. This is relevant not only to obtain access to the actual venue of the negotiations, but also to access particular meetings where various aspects of the texts are being hashed out by government delegations who have a strong stake in the outcome of the documents. Therefore, exclusion—both of governments and members of civil society—is seen as an element of negotiations about which marginalised governments and members of civil society must always be attentive to. However, access is only one of the elements that is contested within this arena. While access to the deliberations should not be discounted as being important, the meaning and substance of participation spans a much wider range of dynamics that will be developed in this chapter.

Whose space? Our space!

The site of my study—the actual locations of UN negotiations—is a highly contested space. As noted in previous chapters, the UN is ultimately a space designated for nation-states. However, members of civil society often point out that member governments must be held accountable to the interests of a range of individuals. Additionally, since its inception, the UN has regularly relied on inputs from NGOs and other members of civil society (Korey 1998; Princen and Finger 1994; Soederberg 2005; Willets 2006). Civil society participants who engage in UN-based processes understand that different rules apply to them—both *de jure* and *de facto*. The rules of access to meetings and participation in the meetings vary according to UN body, but CSOs and IPOs regularly have to assert themselves to engage in *and* to influence UN-based policy-making processes. In many ways, this is not so different for governments who perceive themselves to be in a position of unequal power dynamics vis-à-vis more dominant UN member-states. The politics of inclusion and influence are never absent from UN-based negotiations, regardless of the status of the participant. However, for nation-state actors (those who are accredited through government delegations), the legitimacy of participation in the UN system is taken for granted and greatly streamlined. For civil society, access and participation cannot be assumed as a given.

My research site is also a somewhat nebulous space as not all negotiations take place within the actual meeting chambers. Negotiating sessions are ultimately the culmination of long hours of work that have taken place prior to the delivery of an 'intervention' by a government delegation or organisation. The highly scripted statements that are delivered in negotiating sessions have been carefully crafted with close attention to the language of the pertinent agenda item. 'Progress' within the negotiations is characterised by meeting Chairs as being represented by the ability to remove square brackets from around particular phrases in the text, thus signifying consensus among governments in the room. This sort of progress, which moves at a snail's pace and results in texts replete with caveats and 'voluntary commitments', is met with dismay by members of civil society who see the particular environmental problems being debated (climate, biodiversity loss, or desertification, for example) as requiring far more immediate action. Members of civil society have a very different sense of what 'progress' means in this context and often feel the need to engage in actions that are designed to push governments towards making stronger commitments. Yet 'activism' in this context spans a broad continuum, as some governments that feel marginalised in the debates and members of civil society deploy different strategies that range in scope from those that are highly consistent with the rules of diplomacy to those that are far more consistent with the tradition of activism as we have come to recognise it. The latter is marked by theatrical displays and highly visible critical presence, while the former 'works within the system' by leveraging the tools that are extant within the UN diplomatic modes of operating. Throughout this chapter, based on almost a decade of ethnographic research related to climate negotiations and two decades of research within the context of other UN fora, I provide examples of multiple strategies with the goal of examining the complexity of 'participation' in UN policy-making. The actions and strategies that I have witnessed and participated in illuminate the disjuncture between the 'political reality' of the negotiations (referenced in Chapter 1) and the highly charged sense of exigency experienced by members of civil society.

Using UN-based climate-policy negotiations to provide concrete examples for this analysis, the chapter develops a concept that is often presented as a binary opposition: civil society is either participating, or it is not. Practitioners engaged in global governance and academics who study it are well aware that this characterisation is too simplistic. Thus, the objective in this chapter is to use specific examples derived from actual negotiations in order to explicitly articulate some of the complexities and intricacies of what 'participation' in global governance actually means.

Participation as process

Rather than attempting to answer the question of whether civil society is 'effective' in influencing policy processes related to issues of international importance, I utilise specific deliberations to argue that civil society participation in global governance is not a given but a *process*—one with important implications for individuals who exist in various disparate locations. For example, as I will address in greater detail in Chapter 5, recent debates regarding 'Reducing Emissions from Deforestation and forest Degradation' (or REDD, as it has commonly come to be known in climate-related fora) have immense implications for a host of individuals who have no physical presence in UN deliberations and who are not formally engaged in the policy-making process. As policies related to REDD are being shaped up in the corridors and meeting rooms of larger institutions of global governance such as the UN and the World Bank, the 'worth' of existing forests as carbon sinks or carbon offsets, particularly those in the Global South, has the potential to exacerbate tenuous land-tenure dynamics experienced by forest-dependent peoples (Eastwood 2011b). Thus, CSOs and IPOs engaged in climate negotiations understand that the stakes are high. The high level of political attention that has recently been given to climate-related policy means that civil society participants must be keenly attentive to the shifts in the negotiating terrain. As political forces influence what issues can and cannot be taken up in negotiations, civil society participants understand that they must be strategic about how they respond.

Strategic essentialism and civil society

Indeed, 'civil society' itself is a blanket term that merges a range of individuals with often antithetical positions (Cohen and Arato 1994; Keane 1998, 1988a, 1988b; Seligman 1992). In fact, within the context of UN-based negotiations, an important and political distinction has been made between members of 'civil society' and 'Indigenous Peoples', even though many members of both groups share similar concerns. I address in Chapter 1 the fact that it is problematic to view Indigenous Peoples under the umbrella of 'civil society' given the implication of 'non-governmental' status that comes with that designation. Many of the core issues that Indigenous Peoples have been struggling for within the context of international negotiations, such as self-determination and sovereign rights, are undermined by this designation, as Indigenous Peoples' governance structures preceded the current system of the nation-state on which the UN is predicated. In multiple fora under the UN system, in fact, the term 'Indigenous Peoples' has been rejected by certain member-states, as it has the potential to challenge the sovereignty of the nation-state by codifying the recognition of Indigenous Peoples as distinct, self-governing entities. It is only recently that the term 'Indigenous and local communities' (ILCs) has been transformed to 'Indigenous Peoples and local communities' (IPLCs) within the context of negotiations under the CBD, for example. Yet, even as the term 'civil society' has such levels of politicisation, it also exists as a key reality imbued with the potential to be an agent of both local and global change. Conceptualising the term 'civil society' in line with Spivak's (1987) notion of 'strategic essentialism' posits a critique of the essentialising nature of the category while also maintaining an acknowledgement of the political and strategic utility of that same category. While preserving the critique and the strategic use simultaneously is easier said than accomplished, in the practical lexicon of UN negotiations, 'civil society' tends to represent a point of distinction *from* member-states. In this chapter, I deploy the term 'civil society' to capture this dynamic. However, as strategic allegiances are often drawn between members of CSOs and marginalised governments, some of the examples provided here illustrate that certain dynamics can be leveraged to move the policy process in particular directions. Some of the strategies utilised by participants are more effective than others. Some strategies, as I will discuss in the chapter, threaten the very possibility of access of members of civil society with potentially dire consequences for participation in future deliberations. The examples utilised here are designed to explore these complexities and to provide tools to think through the myriad elements involved in global governance as it pertains to particular aspects of civil society engagement in policy-making processes.

The tensions that arose regarding the participation of civil society in UN-based climate-change negotiations illustrates the complexities of the term that were introduced in Chapter 1. While the tensions surrounding civil society and global governance will not be resolved in any final way, the dynamics unfolding under the UNFCCC-related negotiations present new challenges for both government and non-governmental actors. As participants strategically respond to these challenges, the very terrain of policy-making is transformed, providing a precedent for other negotiations and influencing policy outcomes that impact not only climate change but also the global distribution of resources.

Anticipated and accepted actions

A handout printed to resemble US currency, replete with George Washington himself, proclaiming '650 BILLION A YEAR TO FINANCE CLIMATE CHAOS', attributed to 'Non-Violent Action COP21', with one side in French and the other in English. A large poster with an iconic picture of an Indigenous Person, positioned over the official COP15 logo on a pillar inside the Bella Center, stating (in Spanish) 'Indigenous People are not the problem—they are the solution.' A series of individuals, strategically located along the moving walkway that transports participants into the negotiations in Warsaw at UNFCCC's COP19, holding posters asking participants where *they* will be in 2050 and whether they should consider future generations in their negotiations of climate commitments. These sorts of activism are normal and expected. UN meetings would be missing an important element were actions not held and flyers containing impassioned pleas not distributed. The level of coordination of these actions varies, as does the 'legality' of protest, as some UN bodies require that members of civil society allow the Secretariat to know about any actions and prohibit the posting of any materials without authorisation. For example, at the CBD COP10 in Nagoya, Japan, members of civil society had to seek permission to hold an 'action' outside of the entrance to the venue, and, since no potentially critical materials could be posted, some members of civil society met at a nearby apartment, improvised woodblock carvings out of potatoes, and printed brief but artful statements on post-it notes, which were then stuck to the inside of doors in washroom stalls. This apparently benign action could have been met with critique from governments and the Secretariat—and even sanctions if those who had created and posted the images had been identified, but there was, to my knowledge, no response to this mini-protest. However, this is not always the case, and members of civil society who have been engaged in UN policy-making processes for extended periods of time understand that it is best to engage in more radical actions outside of the context of the venue itself so as not to jeopardise access and participation. This stance can provoke conflict among members of civil society, however, as will be explored later in this chapter. The essential question of whether it is best to 'work within the system' or to engage in more radical actions is one that is not new to social movements. The question of who gets to define the parameters of proper or acceptable actions is likewise one that non-governmental participants in UN fora regularly grapple with.

UNFCCC and the climate movement

Two-week meetings of the UNFCCC COPs are typically accompanied by rallies and marches that take place in the streets around the COP host city. For example, on 12 December 2015, as the world watched negotiators wrangle with deliberations in Paris at COP21, the infamous 'Red Lines' protest took place as the negotiations inside 'Le Bourget' were in their final hours. Organisers of the 'd12' Red Lines protest stated the following in a pamphlet that was distributed among negotiators and participants: 'Our message is simple: a liveable planet is a red line we're prepared to defend.' Taking up the language of negotiators who argue that particular points are their 'red lines', signifying that they are non-negotiable, organisers explicitly intended to engage with the language of the negotiations. This became translated into an undeniably visible display of support for climate action, as thousands of people dressed in red, carrying red flowers, and unfurling red banners, marched through the streets of Paris from the Arc du Triomphe to the Eiffel Tower.

In fact, though, the organisers had planned for a march at the start of the Paris negotiations to take place as well. This was complicated by the French government's response to the 13 November terrorist attacks in Paris, which resulted in the establishment of a state of emergency, thereby effectively making all forms of protest—and even gathering in public spaces in numbers of more than two people—illegal. Not condoned by organisers of the Paris COP21 civil society actions, many people defied the ban and, on 29 November, protesters were met with tear gas and riot police. At least 300 people were arrested, and the remainder of the actions planned for the two-week time period to coincide with the UNFCCC negotiations were thrown into question.

Organisers were in a bind, as the Paris negotiations were deemed to be the most crucial of the COPs since Copenhagen, and civil society presence was imperative to many CSOs and IPOs who had travelled to attend the COP, along with thousands of individuals who had no access to the actual meetings yet were interested in being a part of 'the movement'. The UN climate marches were following on historical landmark marches, such as the People's Climate March that took place in New York City in September 2014. As the UN New York's headquarters hosted the Climate Summit, attended by over 100 world leaders, approximately 400,000 people marched through the streets of Manhattan. Representing over 1,500 organisations that had officially affiliated with the People's Climate March, and hundreds of thousands of individuals who were not affiliated with specific organisations, the march represented a significant moment for climate activism. Both the UN Climate Summit and the march were intended to raise the profile of the Paris climate negotiations that were to take place in 2015. Thus, as concerned individuals converged in Paris for COP21, the state of emergency created significant impediments to legal and effective civil society action.

Organisers responded by continuing to hold trainings for interested individuals. Contained in these trainings were suggestions for legal advice, the repeated importance of maintaining non-violence, and reminders to ensure that people did not congregate anywhere except in pairs so as to not engage in actions that were deemed as being illegal under the state of emergency. Up until the night prior to the previously planned d12 protest, whether or not actions would take place was highly unclear. Organisers continued to negotiate with government officials and law enforcement in the hopes that some middle ground could be established. As I attended one of the informational sessions related to the d12 protests, I was struck by the level of concern that organisers had: not only that their actions be constructive and non-violent but also that their actions should not negatively impact marginalised people in Paris. The original action designed to coincide with the end of the official negotiations was slated to take place around Le Bourget, where the negotiations were being held. However, organisers noted that this location, on the outskirts of Paris, was also where many immigrants lived. They were highly reluctant to bring more police presence to communities that were already being targeted as potentially harbouring terrorists. Thus, the organisers changed the plan and instructed people to arrive at the Arc de Triomphe, and to do so only in twos. We were to wear red, avoid confrontation with law enforcement, and dissipate when necessary.

Fortunately for members of civil society, an agreement was reached between local government and action organisers in the eleventh hour. Word spread quickly that the march was on but that participants were to be especially careful to remain within the bounds of legal activity lest the action be marred by claims that protesters were unruly, counterproductive, or misdirected. The streets around the Arc de Triomphe filled with marchers. I encountered 350.org founder Bill McKibben, scientist-activist Sandra Steingraber, anti-consumerist activist 'Reverend Billy', and Amy Goodman of Democracy Now. I was struck by how far the issues had come since Copenhagen in 2009. Granted, there were similar themes displayed on signs, banners, and clothing. But more apparent in 2015 was the message that fossil fuels needed to be kept in the ground. In fact, it was on the streets of Paris that I realised that the anti-fracking movement—a movement that grew stronger with filmmaker Josh Fox's work on the subject of fracking—was now solidly connected to the climate movement. The 'fractivists', such as John Fenton, of Pavilion, Wyoming, were out in force in Paris. This was a movement that began as a concern for water quality and other health impacts in people's communities. The anti-fracking movement has clearly moved away from 'NIMBYism' and now levels a solid critique at the broader fossil-fuel infrastructure as a result of the impacts of climate change.

Historical precedent: Conflict and action in Copenhagen

A significant dynamic that fuelled civil society action in Paris was the failure of COP15 in Copenhagen to achieve a strong climate commitment. It was clear that, leading into the deliberations at COP15, both governments *and* members of civil society were highly invested in a strong outcome. The topic of the future of the Kyoto Protocol, the only legally-binding element of the Climate Agreement—a protocol that would require countries in the Global North ('Annex I countries') to reduce greenhouse gas (GHG) emissions, was one of the more highly contentious elements. In spite of inspiring speeches made by multiple heads of state at the UN General Assembly Climate Change Summit held at UN headquarters in New York on 22 September 2009, word began to circulate that a 'deal' would not be reached in Copenhagen. This meant that no further legally-binding agreement was likely to be made, and the Kyoto Protocol itself was in jeopardy. Citing the poor global economy as a rationale for moving climate change to the back burner, countries of the Global North balked at the notion of generating a stronger legally-binding agreement on climate change.

Fuelling multiple civil society responses, including the 'Seal the Deal' campaign, the understanding that powerful governments were not willing to take actions that would legally bind them to cut GHGs enraged, enlivened, and galvanised civil society actors. Repeatedly, in Copenhagen, it was stated by civil society participants that what was needed was a 'fair, ambitious, and legally-binding agreement', meaning that the agreement should take into account the 'common but differentiated responsibilities' of countries in the Global North and the Global South, it should include 'ambitious' reduction targets for GHG-emitting countries, *and* it should be legally-binding, rather than a 'soft law' voluntary understanding.

In addition to the contentious point regarding the future of the Kyoto Protocol and the lack of developed countries' commitments, many civil society actors approached the Copenhagen meetings with a concern about the dominant understandings of acceptable limits of actual global warming. For many activists and for the governments representing SIDS, for whom very minor sea-level increases can have catastrophic impacts, a 1.5-degree Celsius increase in average global temperatures should not be exceeded. According to the IPCC Fourth Assessment report, in order to prevent an increase of global temperatures above 1.5 degrees, the total amount of carbon dioxide in the atmosphere cannot exceed 350 parts per million. Participating in climate-related meetings as a bloc of countries, the block of countries known as AOSIS (Alliance of Small Island States) became a focal point for pressures to institutionalise measures that would ensure a maximum global average temperature increase of 1.5 degrees Celsius. However, this was a highly contested point, as governments that were unwilling to commit to cutting GHG emissions—that rely upon a fossil-fuel-based global economy for their domestic economic health—refused to negotiate climate agreements related to a 1.5-degree global temperature increase.

Within the context of concerns about acceptable degree of warming and the future of the Kyoto Protocol, a major uproar was created when a draft alternative to the texts of the two 'tracks'—the AWG-KP and AWG-LCA—was leaked to the British press through *The Guardian*. In an article titled 'Copenhagen: Leaked Draft Deal Widens Rift Between Rich and Poor Nations', *The Guardian* quoted the Sudanese delegate Lumumba Di-Aping as saying, 'This text destroys both the UN Convention on climate change and the Kyoto Protocol. This is aimed at producing a new treaty, a new legal initiative that throws away the basis of [differing] obligations between the poorest and most wealthy nations in the world' (Di-Aping, quoted in Vidal and Milmo 2009). The five-page text, known as the 'Danish text', as it had originated with the Danish delegation, became a major point of contention among governments who felt that the text was an attempt to subvert the process. It was equally poorly received by members of civil society who were concerned about the lack of commitments contained in the new text. UNFCCC Executive Secretary, Yvo de Boer, insisted that the text was intended to simply garner discussion among some of the governments who were trying to bridge difficult gaps in agreement and that the texts from the AWG-KP and AWG-LCA were still the official negotiating texts, but the damage had been done.

Delegates from AOSIS fought back. The lead negotiator for Tuvalu, Ian Fry (who, prior to becoming Tuvalu's negotiator, had been an active NGO member working for Greenpeace), proposed what became known as the 'Tuvalu Protocol', which sent the already tenuous negotiations into a tailspin. There were walkouts by delegations who felt that the Danish text was designed to shut developing countries out of the process and to minimise commitments of Global North nations.

Civil society activists both inside and out of the Bella Center immediately aligned with Tuvalu, with impromptu actions such hastily printed signs that stated 'We Stand with AOSIS' that were held aloft simultaneously by hundreds of participants at a press conference with Bill McKibben of 350.org, Ambassador Antonio Lima of Cape Verde (Vice-President of AOSIS), and Ricken Patel, the Executive Director of Avaaz, one of the most active CSOs in Copenhagen. Signs held by activists outside the Bella Center stated 'Stand with Tuvalu!' and 'Tuvalu is the REAL DEAL'. The draft Danish text became a prism through which years of frustration were refracted as it served as a rallying point for delegates who were disenchanted with the UN process and for civil society members with heightened concerns that governments were simply failing to address an impending environmental crisis.

Access: Shut out of the negotiations

The tensions surrounding the content of the negotiations themselves were compounded by concerns regarding access to the Bella Center after the first week of the negotiations. Many members of civil society came to Copenhagen simply to be a part of what they considered to be a monumental historic event. For example, several journalism students from the Netherlands came to film a documentary that they then planned to take back to their campus. Interviewing people who were coming out of the Bella Center, the students explained that they knew they wouldn't have access to the negotiations but that they wanted to document a piece of important history. These students were not alone. Impromptu and planned actions could be found throughout the city of Copenhagen at all hours of the day and night. Government delegates and other participants streamed between the Bella Center and other activities throughout the city, including a talk given by Nobel Laureate Wangari Maathai on a ship docked in the harbour. While many members of civil society were fully aware that they wouldn't see the inside of the Bella Center except as it was being broadcast to those outside through multiple media, approximately 30,000 members of civil society had legitimately registered to attend and participate in COP15. In addition to the individual countries' delegations, some of which numbered close to 1,000, approximately 40,000 people had registered to attend COP15. Organisers of the meetings were in a bind as they argued that the Bella Center had a capacity of only 11,000 people at any given time.

In this context, the organisers began to institute a 'secondary badge' system for members of civil society. 'Primary badges' were imperative for all participants and could be obtained only by going through the proper mechanisms of gaining access to UN meetings. Security was tight, with several checkpoints and X-ray processes that rivalled even the most strict airline procedures. While there were several significant complaints from members of civil society regarding the 'primary badge' stage of the process in Copenhagen, as lines of participants waiting to obtain their access badges snaked for approximately a kilometre outside of the Bella Center on the frigid morning of 8 December, the allocation of 'secondary badges' at COP15 in Copenhagen created far more contention, as it was seen to be an arbitrary and additional impediment to participation. Thousands of members of civil society who had properly registered for the meetings, obtained accreditation, and travelled to Copenhagen from all points of the globe were finding themselves in the position of having increased their carbon footprint with no formal means to participate in the larger policy process designed to reduce GHG emissions.

Clearly, the UNFCCC Secretariat was in a difficult position. Once UN procedures for admitting members of civil society are established, monitoring the numbers of civil society participants becomes difficult if individuals are legitimately meeting the pre-established criteria for inclusion. However, the lack of access to the Bella Center created a logistical nightmare that served as an important lesson to organisers of future climate change negotiations—with implications for civil society participation, as will be discussed below. However, in Copenhagen, it seems that organisers were taken by surprise by the sheer volume of civil society presence. Meetings of the WTO, the World Bank, and the IMF are typically met with a strong showing of engagement by members of civil society. However, the outpouring of commitment to actively participating in the climate-change negotiations—an option that does not exist in the WTO or other such fora but that ostensibly exists under the UN—presented major problems for negotiation organisers.

One civil society participant posted a publication online decrying the 'Restricted Access—to Planet Earth' (Wittneben 2009). A blogger characterised the event as 'an insane circus' and noted that people had come to Copenhagen with high hopes yet had found themselves 'locked out entirely from the Bella Center due to access restrictions on the last days, showing how the logistical side of COP15 has failed' (christopherbaan 2009). Thus, the 'secondary badge' process became a politicised and somewhat chaotic point of contention for many individuals who were literally shut out of the formal process. However, as members of civil society know, there are multiple ways to participate in policy-related arenas, and access to the actual negotiations is just one of them. As Juan Carlos Soriano, a Peruvian 23-year-old representative of SustainUS stated,

> Our heads of state here came with the positions of what they feel [represents] the majority of their population. In Peru, our position would probably be more progressive if we had a stronger voice from civil society, pushing our government to take leadership on environmental issues. The same thing could be said for the United States.
>
> (Soranio, quoted in Hiskes 2009)

Members of civil society engage in multiple 'spheres of strategy work' that intersect with literal negotiations yet span far beyond the negotiations to include both transnational activism and 'on-the-ground' local-level projects. In fact, being 'shut out' of negotiations can be used strategically to highlight issues surrounding participation and to argue for greater inclusion in future deliberations. In Copenhagen, it became clear that the climate change movement is a force to be reckoned with. CSOs, both inside and outside of the Bella Center, were clear about the fact that they perceived climate change as representing the most important environmental crisis of our time. The Climate Change March that snaked through the city of Copenhagen on 12 December 2009 represented the intensity of the concern that civil society members have about the implications of a changing global climate. March organisers estimated that 100,000 people participated, while Copenhagen police placed the number closer to 30,000. Regardless of actual figures, the march was intended to be a clear rejection of UNFCCC process as it was proceeding among negotiators inside the Bella Center. The juxtaposition of the theatrical and energetic presence of activists with the dispassionate and arcane policy negotiations painted a stark contrast as marchers carried bright placards with such sayings as 'THERE IS NO PLANET B' and, significantly, 'Blah blah blah' in reference to the seemingly endless policy talk going on inside the negotiations.

Copenhagen 'results' and beyond: Continued tensions for civil society

The COP15 meetings ended without resolving the tensions that had been brewing both inside and out of the Bella Center. The 'Danish Text', after its initial bombshell effect on the negotiations, went through several iterations and came out the other side as the 'Copenhagen Accords'—a five-page document that approximately thirty countries signed on to. The 'two tracks'—the Ad-Hoc Working Group on Long-Term Cooperative Action (AWG-LCA) and the Ad-Hoc Working Group on the Kyoto Protocol (AWG-KP) were given an extended mandate to continue their work over the year and to revisit their progress at COP16. Participants involved in the work of the AWG-LCA and AWG-KP met in Bonn in April 2010, and again from 31 May to 11 June 2010. It was at this latter meeting that a series of unanticipated events served to highlight the brewing tensions between activist civil society and UN business as usual. The context for the ultimate blow-up which took place on the last day of the June Bonn negotiations was the level of civil society concern about what had taken place in Copenhagen regarding their inability to access the venue and the apparent discomfort that some governments were feeling about the highly visible, often theatrical and dramatic, civil society presence in Copenhagen. Members of civil society were keen to know how the plans for COP16 would accommodate them, and some governments were apparently anxious about how they could effectively engage in the work of negotiating policy at COP16. At the scheduled briefing of members of civil society by the UNFCCC Executive Secretary, Yvo de Boer, the question was raised regarding what the Secretariat was doing to prevent 'what happened in Copenhagen' (meaning how civil society was largely shut out of the process during the final days of negotiations). De Boer's response was telling in that he stated that the COP16 organisers were trying to get a better sense, through the registration process, of what civil society members' expectations of participation would be. He argued that if an individual's purpose in attending COP16 was to simply 'get a button', then perhaps that should be treated differently than if the person were there to negotiate texts. For de Boer, the solution was to develop 'more sophistication' in the way that 'space is used physically'. Perhaps, de Boer argued, we could use one space for exhibits and another separate space for negotiations.

This model that de Boer was proposing appeared to be the one that was being put into place for COP16, as details about the venue were become clearer to participants of the Bonn meetings in June. That the COP16 meetings would be taking place in Mexico had already raised some concerns for members of civil society who were worried about how the Mexican government and law enforcement would deal with the types of activities that civil society had engaged in during the Copenhagen meetings. Then, as details were revealed about the venue in Mexico, civil society participants developed new concerns. It turned out that the actual negotiations were being planned to take place in an all-inclusive resort in Cancun and that only state delegations could reserve rooms at the resort. The plan was to have exhibits and side events taking place at another location—a 'fairground' that was yet to be constructed—several kilometres away from the actual policy discussions.

While this model of geographical separation of policy negotiation and side events worked towards solving the problems that organisers in Copenhagen experienced in terms of sheer numbers of participants overwhelming the venue, it assumes two key elements that must be addressed in thinking through the complexities of civil society participation in global governance. First, it assumes that there is a clear distinction between members of civil society who are engaged in the actual policy-negotiation process and those who simply want to be part of a larger event (to 'pick up a button', in de Boer's terms, for example). Second, it assumes that 'participation' is merely textual and documentary and *not* theatrical, dramatic, or intentionally disruptive. A clear tactic of civil society members in Copenhagen was to attempt to interrupt the talk of policy negotiations by throwing what they perceived to be the 'real issues' into the faces of the negotiators—in ways that clearly made some governments uncomfortable.

What a difference half a degree makes

This tension came to a head on the last two days of negotiations in Bonn in June 2010. The issue that sparked the controversy was one that presented a clear point of contention for civil society participants. During meetings related to the SBSTA (Subsidiary Body for Scientific and Technological Advice), a particular issue under 'Agenda Item 9: Scientific, technical and socio-economic aspects of mitigation of climate change' became highly contentious. The schedule in Bonn had established that Agenda Item 9 would be addressed on Wednesday, 9 June. However, when some government delegations intervened to ask the Secretariat to prepare a technical report that would assess the implications of a range of global temperature increases, including a 1.5 degree Celsius increase, the debate became protracted. Many oil-producing states, such as Saudi Arabia, Oman, and Qatar, voiced serious concerns. The discussion became so contentious that the meeting could not conclude the agenda item and was scheduled to be resumed the following day. At the resumed discussion on Thursday, 10 June, it became apparent that the opposing governments were not going to agree to ask the Secretariat to compile the report—this was their 'red line'. Venezuela, in support of compiling the report, made the first intervention in the meeting, noting that Venezuela understood that 'various Parties had expressed concerns about the Chair's preparation of a technical paper'. However, Venezuela went on to argue that the preparation of such a paper 'could help us to move forward' and address the contentious issues with the assistance of scientific evidence. Saudi Arabia immediately followed with an intervention opposing Venezuela's statement. The delegate from Saudi Arabia stated that

> We listened very carefully to our colleague from Venezuela with regard to her proposal, but I would like to announce that we would strongly object to have any conclusion on this matter. We can take this up in Cancun [at COP16] ... [T]here is no consensus, and even if we stay until tomorrow evening, there will be no consensus.

This intervention was followed by Oman, who stated that:

> [M]y delegation believes that the objective achievement of 2 degrees Celsius has scientific justification as was clarified in the Fourth Assessment Report of the IPCC. My delegation also believes that we have not reached the right time to discuss this issue, and we can return to the topic at COP16.

Kuwait then spoke in support of the interventions made by both Saudi Arabia and Oman. This was followed by an intervention by Qatar, who stated that '[M]y delegation believes that the IPCC is the best scientific frame of reference as was stated by Oman. This is not the time to discuss this. It can be addressed in Cancun.'

Given the fact that the 1.5 degree Celsius increase had been such a point of importance for civil society participants in Copenhagen, the negotiations unfolding under Agenda Item 9 of the SBSTA were not well received by CSOs. Some members of civil society explained to me that the position of Saudi Arabia, Qatar, Oman, and Kuwait was related to those governments' concern that, as the IPCC prepared its Fifth Assessment Report, 1.5 degrees might become the new 'baseline'. This would have implications for the dominant agreed-upon scientific evidence regarding acceptable limits of climate change. As their domestic economies rely heavily on a fossil-fuel-based global economy, the four Parties were working on various fronts to weaken the policy texts. Civil society participants in the Bonn meetings incorporated their concerns about the SBSTA debates into their actions and activism at the meetings. The organisation 'CAN', or Climate Action Network, awarded its 'Fossil of the Day Award' to Saudi Arabia on 9 June and came out strongly against Saudi Arabia's position regarding the SBSTA debate in its 10 June issue of *Eco*, a double-sided flyer that reports on the daily events. In an article called 'Cut the Nonsense', CAN wrote:

> With an issue as serious as the survival of entire nations, you would think all governments would be able to negotiate the matter seriously and in good faith. However, as last night's teeth-rattling exercise in negotiations dentistry showed, even agreeing a technical report about potential 1.5°C scenarios is not immune. During the SBSTA evening session, Saudi Arabia managed to plow through every possible diversion, suggesting for instance that vulnerable countries just use Google if they want more knowledge about the scientific findings relating to their survival, or that it is beyond the capacity of the Secretariat to produce a summary of recent scientific studies.
>
> (CAN 2010)

The commentary voiced in the *Eco* publication was not controversial. In fact, it was expected that civil society would be critical of Saudi Arabia's position in the negotiations. However, the discontent with Saudi Arabia fuelled other actions by civil society participants in Bonn that served to bring tensions between member-states and civil society participation to a head. Apparently, on the evening of Thursday, 10 June 2010, some members of civil society retrieved the name placard of Saudi Arabia from one of the negotiating rooms. During the negotiations, the placards are used to demarcate where delegations should sit, and they are also raised by delegations when they want to be called upon by the Chair to make an intervention. Thus, placards are as iconic representations of UN negotiations as interpretation earpieces or UN-logo flags. After the civil society individuals obtained Saudi Arabia's placard, they broke it into several pieces, placed it in one of the toilets at the UN meeting venue, and photographed the broken placard in the toilet. This action, while consistent with a certain level of civil society activism that attempts to push boundaries and call 'business as usual' into question, clearly crossed the line of acceptable actions within the context of UN negotiations. While the vast majority of civil society actions in recent climate-change negotiations may have been seen as merely entertaining or somewhat theatrical by government delegates, this particular incident was roundly criticised by government delegates and members of civil society alike.

Negotiations derailed: Participation jeopardised

In fact, denunciation of this action by government delegations occupied the majority of what was intended to be a closing Plenary on Friday, 11 June 2010.[1] During this session, it was revealed that the desecration of Saudi Arabia's placard had taken place, although the details were not described in full, and at this point I was unaware of the incident, as were many members of civil society. Multiple governments came out with interventions in opposition to this sort of behaviour. The Chair of the session first gave the floor to Mexico, who had requested the opportunity to make a statement on behalf of the Bureau of the COP. When Mexico took the floor, the delegate stated:

> I have the honour to speak on behalf of the COP15/MOP5 Bureau in regard to some incidents that took place inside the UN conference premises which intended to put pressure on certain Parties. We want to refer in particular to the destruction and misuse of a country plate to produce an image, one which goes beyond any acceptable behaviour. We strongly condemn such acts and highlight the importance of mutual respect to diversity of opinions, as well as sensitivity to civil norms. We also want to thank the Secretariat for launching an investigation and look forward for an appropriate action to steam [sic] out this type of behaviour. I am sure I can speak on behalf, not only of the Bureau, but of all Parties, all participants, in calling for the enhancement of the level of the debate and public manifestations regardless of our differences. It is essential to maintain an atmosphere conducive to open, respectful, and fruitful negotiations and dialogue.

Australia then took the floor and thanked the Chair and the Bureau for their statements. The Australian delegate, on behalf of a group of countries known as 'the Umbrella Group', stated that the Umbrella Group 'considers the disrespect given to a country here to be deeply regrettable'. These statements were followed by multiple interventions by individual member-states as well as delegates who were representing blocs, such as AOSIS. Turkey took the floor and stated that '[W]e believe that it is totally unacceptable to stage such attacks on the moral values of any member-states ... and I hope that the authorities will do everything possible to clarify this incident.' The delegate from China then took the floor and stated the following:

> The Chinese delegation fully supports the statement by the representative from Mexico on behalf of the Bureau. We think this incident is very serious, and it took place in the UN conference premises. It shouldn't have happened. We sincerely hope that all Parties including the Secretariat and the organizers should pay full attention to such an incident so as to take necessary measure avoid the recurrence of such an incident. We feel that our conference needs a good atmosphere so that we can promote our negotiations. Our task is still very heavy. We sincerely hope that we can work in an atmosphere of friendship and comfort ... so as to have a meaningful and resultful [sic] negotiations.

The Chair took the floor to ask delegates to move on from the topic and address the scheduled agenda items, noting that there was significant repetition in delegates' statements. However, member-states were not finished discussing the issue, and interventions condemning the event continued. Lebanon took the floor to point to a separate action by members of civil society that had also taken place the night before. The delegate from Lebanon stated:

> [T]he flag of Saudi Arabia was also held yesterday [in the corridors] and it was treated without much respect. I would have made this intervention if it was the flag of any other nation as well. However, particularly the flag of Saudi Arabia has religious words written on it, so we can be funny, creative, innovative and display all of our ideas in [a] way which we respect. But this still has to be done under the frame of respect and diplomacy. We are under the United Nations meetings.

Switzerland then took the floor 'to associate, for our group also ... with what has been said by Mexico on behalf of the Bureau. Mutual respect is very important for the whole process inside the process itself—also outside the process. Without mutual respect, it is not possible to achieve any results.' This was followed by an intervention by Egypt, who associated with the previous speakers, and stated that, 'I would support the point raised by Turkey that this incident has to be accounted for, and there is security here—there are authorities that are responsible for that—and we would look forward for an explanation in the next session on who is responsible [for] this despicable act.' The interventions continued, coming from multiple countries, punctuated at points by the Chair's request to move on from the subject and address the scheduled agenda items. But clearly the event had struck a nerve. Venezuela referenced the incident as an 'act against the sovereignty of a member country'. Mali, too, referenced the fact that 'each Party is sovereign in the negotiations' and that 'it is vital to do everything to avoid such a situation ... it is a matter of the sovereignty of our organisation'. Many of the delegates utilised the double meaning of the words 'environment' and 'atmosphere' to argue for a 'positive' or 'healthy' negotiating environment, as they deliberated environmental policy. Kuwait even stated that 'We are here to protect the environment, whereas others are disturbing the environment.' Several interventions called for investigation as to who was responsible for the incident, and strong actions to be taken. The references to the 'investigation', 'security', and the primacy of the notion of nation-state 'sovereignty' were designed to highlight the tenuous nature of civil society presence within the walls of official UN business. While the intervention from Lebanon had referenced the 'innovative' and 'creative' elements of civil society actions, it was clear that rules of engagement had been breached. The standard diplomacy of UN deliberations, where even dissenting opinions and statements by governments are often phrased in terms that sound positive and encouraging, was thrown into disarray by the events of the previous evening.

As the interventions condemning the act continued, members of civil society began to be concerned that the events would provide a justification for further civil society marginalisation. Given the concerns about the COP16 venue, on behalf of which the Mexican government had initially spoke, providing a solid foundation for critique of civil society presence at the Bonn meetings, and lack of clarity regarding how civil society might gain access to the future negotiations, participants witnessing the stream of interventions during the Plenary on the final day of the Bonn negotiations knew that there needed to be some civil society response to the stream of interventions that had sidelined the actual intended agenda items. The concern was further compounded by the second intervention made by the delegation of China. The delegate apologised for taking the floor a second time but wanted to emphasise the importance of the issue at hand. He stated the following:

[F]or the Chinese, we believe that we should think about the incident from several approaches, that is to draw lessons. The Chinese leader, Chairman Mao, used to say that we should strengthen discipline so that we can forever win in our Revolution. This is a very a very philosophical statement, for discipline within the venue and the rules in the venue, if not fully applied and observed, it is not strange to have such incidents happening. I remember that during the Copenhagen conference ... we see that reporters ... talk[ed] about information from the closed meeting of the UN. The Secretariat should also investigate this incident .... The rules in the UN conference meetings are very clear. If the meeting is a closed one, all participants in the meeting have the moral and legal responsibility without prior approval by the Parties [not] to disclose to outsiders the content of the meeting ... such incident will bring serious negative impact. These two incidents are separate but they are of the same serious nature. I hope that the Secretariat and the Bureau will take measures to ensure that the basic rules of the venue are observed.

Under this one intervention, two issues were conflated to highlight tensions that emerged between Parties themselves in Copenhagen, and the tensions that emerged between Parties and civil society members in Bonn. The association of the incident of the placard with the incident of leaked draft texts to *The Guardian* in Copenhagen at once linked the two contentious situations and also served to heighten calls for 'action' to combat 'unacceptable' behaviour. Additionally, multiple interventions made reference to the case involving the Saudi Arabian flag, the details of which were very unclear. Significantly, what was originally presented as one isolated incident perpetrated by some members of civil society quickly expanded to become plural 'acts of disrespect', in spite of the fact that most participants were not clear about the details regarding the Saudi Arabian flag *or*, in fact, the placard in the toilet. The focus of the interventions shifted from a condemnation of the placard desecration and began to focus on the desecration of the flag of a member-state. As the interventions condemning the incident(s) proceeded for approximately another forty minutes, civil society members present in the meeting grew increasingly concerned. Not only was the issue expanding to include a range of sensitive issues, but it began to take on elements of exclusion. Saudi Arabia took the floor to express appreciation for the support shown by other delegations. The delegate stated that:

[W]hen I raised this point at the Bureau meeting, I wanted to say that what actually happened to Saudi Arabia could of course happen to anyone—to any other country—and we have to prevent any repetition of this sort of thing. We are here as negotiators on behalf of our countries, and we are all trying to move towards an acceptable result. This deliberate harmful act will of course not make any country change its position ... many countries have taken the floor to express their consternation and their condemnation of the action against Saudi Arabia yesterday. In speaking, they were well aware that this was supposed to be a sort of pressure exerted on a country, but would not prevent any country, in fact, from defending its position as everyone looks forward to a consensus solution for everyone ... in the light of what has been said in the Bureau and in the Plenary, we look forward to the results of the investigation and what measures may be imposed to ensure that such things are not repeated in the future.

Here it was made clear that Saudi Arabia would not be pressured by actions by civil society. The very question of whether activism creates social change was being brought into the discussion, at the same time as the presence of civil society was being roundly critiqued.

Damage control

Members of multiple organisations, under the auspices of CAN, quickly mobilised a statement and requested the floor. The Chair recognised the CAN representative as wishing to make a statement on behalf of civil society. The statement represented a keen understanding of the negotiations and the politics of the interventions that had been made. The CAN representative started by saying that her statement was being made on behalf of environmental NGOs, trade-union NGOs, business NGOs, and youth focal points. All four of these categories are recognised as legitimate groupings of CSOs under the UNFCCC. It was a strategic move to gain the support of a range of legitimately recognised NGOs. She went on to state that:

[M]utual respect is fundamental to civil society engagement, and we respect the UNFCCC and all Parties to the Convention. The NGO community members value the UNFCCC process and the relationships we have with the Parties and the negotiators. It seems that emotions may have run high yesterday, and as all involved in this process are concerned for the future existence and wellbeing of the vulnerable countries and peoples, these emotions appear to have led to an incident. We trust that this incident will not divert the attention of Parties from the vitally important work of this Convention. We remain fully committed to working with the Parties to help them achieve an outcome in the UNFCCC that sets us on a path to avoid dangerous interference with climate systems. We appreciate the efforts made by the Secretariat and the Parties in recent ... deliberations to include civil society in this process. We will continue our constructive and productive engagement in this process.

Through this statement, civil society representatives demonstrated a keen awareness of the process and politics. They skilfully avoided either taking ownership of or disavowing the incident but provided a larger context within which the incident should be viewed. They utilised the rhetoric of respect and collaboration to effectively and emphatically argue that they would maintain a presence in the negotiations. Additionally, by referencing the 'concerns for the future and wellbeing of vulnerable countries and peoples', they diplomatically made reference to the origin of the dispute, which involves civil society activism around the potential of a greater than 1.5 degree Celsius increase in global temperatures.

Maintaining a presence: Civil society and continued participation in UNFCCC

As the above exchange illustrates, the politics of civil society participation in global governance are never far from the surface in institutions where policies are negotiated. The UN system continues to produce heated exchanges, as it maintains a commitment to civil society engagement at the same time as it represents the very tenet of sovereignty of the nation-state. While some policy conflicts seem to polarise governments in opposition to each other, aligning some governments with CSOs, other conflicts operate to polarise civil society from member-states. Throughout the deliberation processes, members of civil society work strategically to maintain their presence and to influence policy outcomes. In terms of policy-making in relation to climate change, these issues will clearly not be resolved in any final way at any time soon. After the great disappointment of Copenhagen, the new focus was on the possibility of developing a strong agreement in Cancun at COP16. However, in an effort to avoid the dynamics that arose in Copenhagen, as was mentioned earlier, COP16 was strategically organised to use geography and official transportation to minimise conflict. Many CSOs and IPOs who were following particular parts of the negotiations felt pulled in a variety of different directions. A new 'quota' system has been instituted to ensure that meetings will not be marred by the same conflicts that took place in Copenhagen. By the time of the meetings in Lima, Peru (2014), CSOs and IPOs were allocated fewer spaces than they had been in the past. To date, access to the meetings has been extremely difficult to obtain, with accredited CSOs and IPOs being given a certain number of 'spaces' for both the first and second week of the negotiations during each COP. This was particularly relevant in Paris as members of civil society became highly engaged in levelling a strong critique at governments' inaction on climate. By Paris, civil society members understood that their participation outside of the venue was equally— if not more—important as their participation within the meeting halls. In spite of the state of emergency, actions in Paris reflected the growing concern that clear government action needed to be taken and that the science was becoming increasingly clear. Activists paid close attention to the state of the negotiations and regularly weighed in on whether governments were achieving necessary consensus. As the first draft of the final negotiating text was released, 350.org Executive Director, May Boeve, wrote the following statement. which was posted on the main website for the d12 protest:

> The final text still has some serious gaps. We're very concerned about the exclusion of the rights of indigenous peoples, the lack of finance for loss and damage, and that while the text recognizes the importance of keeping global warming below 1.5 degrees C, the current commitments from countries still add up to well over 3 degrees of warming. These are red lines we cannot cross. After Paris, we'll be redoubling our efforts to deliver the real solutions that science and justice demand.
>
> (Boeve 2015)

It is clear that seasoned members of CSOs and IPOs are savvy as to how best to engage in environmental deliberations that take place under the UN. In this chapter, I've merely touched on the types of activism that CSOs and IPOs engage in and illustrated some examples where the sense of urgency that is felt by people who are not beholden to government 'red lines' causes intense frustration for activists. In the chapters that follow, I continue to address this disjuncture between the goals and interests of civil society, and those of governments, as participants strategically engage in policy-making based on a range of very different— and at times—diametrically opposed—interests.

Note

1 The quotations contained in this segment of the paper come from statements made by participants in the Ad Hoc Working Group on Long-term Cooperative Action (AWG-LCA) during its meeting at 11.00 a.m. on Friday, 11 June 2010, at the UNFCCC venue in Bonn, Germany. The statements have been transcribed verbatim, with deviations from actual terms used noted in the text.

References

Boeve, M. (2015) untitled, available at http://d12.paris/ (accessed 12 July 2018).

Chatterjee, P. and Finger, M. (1994) *The Earth Brokers: Power, Politics and World Development*, London and New York: Routledge.

Christopherbaan (2009) 'COP15 in Retrospect, and Our Common Future', posted for WSC-SD Climate Blog, 21 December, available at http://cop15.wscsd.org/2009/12/21/cop15-in-retrospect-and-our-common-future/ (accessed 13 July 2010).

Climate Action Network (CAN) (2010) 'Cut the Nonsense', *Eco: NGO Newsletter*, 10 June, available at www.climatenetwork.org/eco/bonn-ii-2010-ecos/Bonn%20II%20Eco%2010.pdf (accessed 10 August 2010).

Cohen, J. and A. Arato (1994) *Civil Society and Political Theory*, Cambridge, MA: MIT Press.

Eastwood, L.E. (2011a) 'Climate Change Negotiations and Civil Society Participation: Shifting and Contested Terrain', *Theory in Action: Journal of the Transformative Studies Institute*, 4(1): 8–42.

Eastwood, L.E. (2011b) 'Resisting Dispossession: Indigenous Peoples, the World Bank, and the Contested Terrain of Policy', *New Global Studies*, 5(1): 1–33.

Hiskes, J. (2009) 'There Will Be No Decision about Us, Without Us', *Grist: A Beacon in the Smog*, 19 December, available at www.grist.org/chapter/2009-12-19-peruvian-youth-copenhagen-climate/ (accessed 9 July 2010).

Keane, J. (1988a) *Civil Society and the State: New European Perspectives*, London and New York: Verso.

—— (1988b) *Democracy and Civil Society: On the Predicaments of European Socialism, the Prospects for Democracy, and the Problem of Controlling Social and Political Power*, London; New York: Verso.

—— (1998) *Civil Society: Old Images, New Visions*, Stanford, CA: Stanford University Press.

Korey, W. (1998) *NGOs and the Universal Declaration of Human Rights*, New York: St. Martin's Press.

Princen, T. and M. Finger (1994) *Environmental NGOs in World Politics: Linking the Local and the Global*, London and New York: Routledge.

Seligman, A.B. (1992) *The Idea of Civil Society*, New York: The Free Press.

Soederberg, S. (2005) 'Recasting Neoliberal Dominance in the Global South? A Critique of the Monterrey Consensus', *Alternatives*, 30 (3): 325–64.

Spivak, G. (1987) *In Other Worlds: Essays in Cultural Politics*, London and New York: Routledge.

Vidal, J. and D. Milmo (2009) 'Copenhagen: Leaked Draft Deal Widens Rift Between Rich and Poor Nations', *The Guardian*, 9 December, available at www.guardian.co.uk/environment/2009/dec/09/copenhagen-summit-danish-text-leak (accessed 9 August 2010).

Willetts, P. (2006) 'The Cardoso Report on the UN and Civil Society: Functionalism, Global Corporatism, or Global Democracy?' *Global Governance*, 12(3): 305–24.

Wittneben, B. (2009) 'Restricted Access—to Planet Earth', *Climatico: Independent Analysis of Climate Policy*, available at www.climaticoanalysis.org/post/tag/bella-center/ (accessed 9 July 2010).

4 Civil society engagement in regulating biotechnology under the UN

> We are democratizing creation. Cells are nothing more than a computer, running a program and the program is the genetic code. The code is DNA. The software are the chromosomes. The hardware is the wetware.
>
> (Omri Amirav-Drory, quoted in Cutler 2013)

This story begins with policy-makers, environmentalists, and scientists negotiating an international legally-binding agreement on biological diversity in the late 1980s. The plot, however, takes some unexpected turns—into the realm of high-stakes legal cases, technologically sophisticated genetic research, and computer-generated genetic codes, as Omri Amirav-Drory, founder and CEO of Genome Compiler Corporation articulates in the epigraph to this chapter. Several decades ago, as individuals in disparate locations were converging to generate texts that would come to be the UN CBD, they could not have anticipated the full range of issues that would eventually come to impact both the physical reality of biological diversity and the policy-making terrain that surrounds it. While the original policy texts signed at the 1992 UNCED demonstrate that individuals involved in the policy-making process *were* able to predict many of the issues that would lie ahead, a confluence of significant factors has created a policy terrain related to biological diversity that is very different than it was in 1992.

In many ways, the participants negotiating the CBD in the lead-up to the UNCED negotiations could not have known how the very concept of 'biological diversity' would take future negotiators so far into the convoluted and contentious world of intellectual property rights, the highly technical world of synthetic biology, and the well-funded world of agricultural and pharmaceutical corporate interests. Indeed, these dynamics speak to the current context of a twenty-first-century globalised economy in significant ways. By contrast, comprised primarily of government delegates in ministries of environment and biologists specialising in ecology and other biological sciences, the negotiators of the original text of the CBD in the late 1980s (with the UNEP Governing Council decision 14/26, which called upon UNEP to convene an Ad-Hoc Working Group of experts on biological diversity) and up to the signing of the CBD by governments in 1992, were focused on creating a policy document that would address loss in biological diversity—one of the key environmental issues that was, at that time, emerging as a *global* rather than simply a regional or local problem.

It was clear to negotiators that there would be some contentious issues, given the fact that Article 1 of the Convention sets up the objectives of the CBD as

> the conservation of biological diversity, the sustainable use of its components and the fair and equitable sharing of the benefits arising out of the utilization of genetic resources, including by appropriate access to genetic resources and by appropriate transfer of relevant technologies, taking into account all rights over those resources and to technologies, and by appropriate funding.
>
> (UNEP 1992)

These objectives, which at first glance appear fairly straightforward, outline the scope of the Convention and required significant and time-consuming negotiations to reach this final stage to be signed at UNCED, in Rio de Janeiro, Brazil. The three objectives outlined in Article 1 (conservation, sustainable use, and fair and equitable sharing of benefits) have provided the context for subsequent, often contentious, negotiations over the past 25 years since UNCED. Policy negotiators are well aware that the devil is in the detail—how, for example, do we define what it means for the 'sharing of benefits' to be equitable and fair? What, in fact, does the term 'sustainable' actually mean when applied to real contexts involving loss of biological diversity? Which 'diversity' do we value as being worthy of being saved? How do we measure commitments and success or failure?

All of these are legitimate questions that clearly fall within the purview of the original text. All of these questions are ones that have required protracted debate by governments over the past 25 years. However, as the cases that have emerged subsequently in CBD negotiations demonstrate, the sorts of dynamics that caused debate and contention leading up to the Rio conference in 1992 comprised only a small part of the terrain that would need to be addressed by policy-makers as they engaged in the deliberations under various agenda items over the subsequent years. Unanticipated issues have arisen as being salient ones for negotiators since UNCED in ways that raise important questions about the role of science in policy, the implications of the confluence of corporate and government interests, the fine line between intellectual and physical property, and the ability for more or less powerful actors to influence policy outcomes.

While one theme of this book is that these are always key questions for the intergovernmental environmental policy processes, the particular cases related to negotiations addressing biotechnology, synthetic biology, and, subsequently, 'digital sequencing information', as they were brought into the CBD negotiations, allow for a specific elaboration of these dynamics grounded in actual deliberations. In this chapter, I use a particular instance of several days of text negotiation that took place in Nagoya, Japan, at the tenth COP of the CBD in October 2010 in order to ground the analysis. I then analyse more recent debates that demonstrate how the technical elements of the circumstances have changed, yet members of civil society bring many of the same concerns to the deliberations.

The goal in this chapter is twofold. On the one hand, I'm interested in further illustrating the actual work of policy-making that is obscured in 'final' texts. As I have argued throughout this book, what it means to 'negotiate' policy merits explanation that ethnographic methods are well suited to explore. In attempting to achieve this goal, I draw on the data I gathered within the context of the deliberations that have taken place under the auspices of the CBD over the past decade. I use the technique of providing 'ethnographic snippets' that are designed to bring the reader into the experience of being present in the research site. Additionally, though, through the use of these actual cases, I am interested in contributing to broader discussions regarding the role of science in policy, the implications for civil society participation in global environmental governance, and the confluence of corporate and government objectives at this current juncture. Again, the specific instances of negotiations are intended to provide windows into the embodied realities of these broader dynamics—dynamics that are often reduced to abstract discussions of 'global environmental governance'.

To provide a context for the issues that arose around some of the agenda items that were being addressed at CBD COP10 and the more recent discussions at SBSTTA 22 (the 22nd meeting of the Subsidiary Body on Scientific, Technical and Technological Advice), I sketch out some of the key elements related to the history of these issues in the CBD process, discuss some of the current dynamics associated with relevant legal and scientific developments, address the various interests brought to the table by both state and non-state actors, and illustrate the relevant linkages between the CBD and other policy-making fora. I don't intend for this chapter to represent a comprehensive treatment of any of the above dynamics. It is important to note that the history of the agenda items on which I focus in this chapter is much more complex than will be addressed here. In fact, readers should begin to get a sense of the convoluted and multisited nature of any of the 'cross-cutting' issues dealt with under the auspices of UN negotiations. This assertion is in line with one of the primary points that my analysis is intended to make: in the process of attempting to strategically engage in UN policy-making processes, participants find themselves drawn into a range of policy processes that span across several different bureaucratic and jurisdictional boundaries. While this complexity can sometimes work at odds with various actors' interests, as I will illustrate below, attempts to defer decisions to other arenas are often used (particularly by governments) as a way of achieving an agreement without exceeding mandates. Likewise, non-state actors have often made reference to agreed-upon language of other negotiating fora in order to argue for more robust agreements. In other words, rather than reducing the complexity of agenda items, negotiations of texts often open up a range of issues that serve to transform the policy terrain in important ways. Participants shape policy transformations and also respond strategically in order to effectively engage in the negotiations.

Background of the CBD

As was addressed in Chapter 2, the CBD was one of the three legally binding agreements adopted at the 1992 'Earth Summit' in Rio de Janeiro, Brazil, along with the UNFCCC and the UN Convention to Combat Desertification. The text of the original biodiversity-related agreement itself includes a preamble, forty-two Articles, and three annex segments. As indicated above, the Convention is predicated on expanding upon and further specifying three primary objectives: 'the conservation of biological diversity, the sustainable use of its components and the fair and equitable sharing of the benefits arising out of the utilisation of genetic resources' (UNEP 1992). The Convention entered into force in 1993 and currently (2018) has 196 Parties to the Convention, which means not only that 196 nation-states have signed on to the Convention but that their governments have subsequently ratified it. Parties to the Convention (in addition to observers and other officially recognised and accredited stakeholders) meet every 2 years at COP meetings, which span two weeks of negotiations designed to address various agenda items related to the original goals and objectives of the Convention.

In addition to COPs, the CBD carries out its work in multiple other arenas, such as those organised around 'Working Groups' on various elements contained in the original Convention. The CBD's SBSTTA and 'Subsidiary Body on Implementation' (SBI) meet approximately two times per year to address relevant issues in contribution to the work of the Convention. SBSTTA and SBI meetings are marked by negotiations of texts which are then intended to be fed into the CBD COPs. Additionally, the IPBES was recently established (2012) in order to 'synthesize, review, assess and critically evaluate relevant information and knowledge generated worldwide by governments, academia, scientific organizations, non-governmental organizations and indigenous communities' in relation to 'the state of the planet's biodiversity, its ecosystems and the essential services they provide to society' (IPBES n.d.).

Biodiversity: The CBD and the policy–ideology–science nexus

The term 'biodiversity', a conjunction of the terms 'biological' and 'diversity' often associated with biologist E.O. Wilson (1988), provides a fascinating example of the intersections between science and ideology. David Takacs' (1996) analysis of the term 'biodiversity' in his book *The Idea of Biodiversity: Philosophies of Paradise* displays many of the ideological underpinnings of a concept which has come to be closely associated with the environmental sciences, yet which, as Takacs analyses, also has far more complexity than can be contained under the umbrella of scientific objectivity. Takacs' project is to display how 'biodiversity' developed as an idea and how it has come to take on the aura of a scientific concept, in spite of the fact that it is, in actuality, highly ideologically based. Interestingly, much like the term 'nature', or 'ecosystem', the term 'biodiversity' is a word which ultimately has very nebulous meanings which have been made largely invisible through its association with the discourse and practice of science. Again, this was largely not recognised by scientists and policy-makers leading up to the UNCED negotiations, yet has contributed to the context of contentious debates that have emerged under subsequent CBD negotiations.

Through his interviews with the scientists involved in studying 'biodiversity', Takacs reveals the lack of a cohesive, objective definition for the word. Close attention to the assumptions portrayed in the following sections taken from Takacs' interviews of prominent scientists displays this dynamic. For example, when asked to define 'biodiversity', Peter Brussard stated the following: 'The standard definition is species diversity, and then diversity of communities or habitats that the species combine into, and then, on the other side of the scale, the genetic diversity that the species are comprised of' (quoted in Takacs 1996: 48). Here we see a very clear articulation of the full range of dynamics that cause current CBD negotiations to range off into a wide variety of areas. From species, to habitats, to 'communities' (in the ecosystem biology/ conservation ecology sense), to even genetic material, this wide-ranging definition creates a significantly complex mandate for the CBD. Also interviewed by Takacs, biologist David Ehrenfeld had this to say about defining biodiversity:

> [I]t obviously means to some people species diversity; other people expand on that to include populations. To other people it means genetic diversity, heterozygosity, allelic diversity, often within populations. To many people it means a variety of ecotypes or eco-system types, landscape types. Obviously, it's all of those things ... I think it's one of those wonderful catchwords like *sustainable development,* that, because it's vaguely defined, has a broad appeal, like motherhood.
>
> (Takacs 1996: 48)

Interestingly, Ehrenfeld clearly recognised the ideological slippages that are inherent in the nebulous nature of the term 'biodiversity'. The fact that it is an entity that is 'vaguely defined', according to Ehrenfeld, clearly creates the context for more than the usual complexity for MEA negotiators. Takacs quotes Daniel Janzen as indicating that biodiversity is '[t]he whole package of genes, populations, species, and the cluster of interactions that they manifest' (1996: 49). Thus, if biodiversity is 'the whole package of genes', etc., to take Janzen's definition, and if it actually even includes 'the cluster of interactions that they manifest', then what does it mean to preserve it? Are we truly interested in preserving *all* of biodiversity, when we go about researching antibiotics or enact programmes to eradicate 'invasive species'? When policy-makers are mandated to address the loss of biological diversity, what, exactly, are they mandated to do? How could one ever—never mind an entire room full of governments with differing interests—come to some sort of agreement as to how to arrest the loss of biological diversity? And what happens when humans *create* biological diversity? Clearly, the terrain of CBD negotiations is fraught with inevitable tensions and conflicts, only some of which will be addressed in this chapter.

In 1992, 'biological diversity' was acknowledged by negotiators, scientists, and policy-makers as being under threat of degradation and therefore in need of a broader policy response. It was evident that human activities were impacting species extinction to the extent that scientists had genuine cause for concern. Not only are engaged individuals concerned about the loss of 'charismatic megafauna', such as tigers, elephants, or polar bears, but ecologists understand the importance of the full range of contributors to the health of an ecosystem. Like a Jenga game, removing blocks only works for so long before the entire tower tumbles. This sense of urgency allowed those engaged in the original debates that produced the texts for the CBD to push through potential conflicts and to generate the Convention that provided a scaffolding for the negotiations that were to follow in Working Groups, Subsidiary Bodies, and COPs. However, one of the dynamics that was acknowledged by early policy-makers and scientists—that 'biodiversity' also included the actual genetic level of organisms—provides the basis for the negotiations that are addressed in this chapter.

Synthetic biology: Human intervention in genetic codes

Humans have been modifying the genetic material of organisms for over 10,000 years as a central part of the intentional cross-breeding of particular plant and animal species for agriculture. However, the modification of recombinant DNA, which has required sophisticated technology and laboratory equipment, is a recent phenomenon that has garnered attention in multiple arenas, both within the UN policy-making process and outside of these deliberations. Biotechnology is an arena that has seen rapid technological advances in industry and scientific research sectors over the past couple of decades. It has become clear that changes in genetic material can have the potential to impact the physical reality of biological diversity in significant ways, as will be elaborated on later in this chapter. 'Biotechnology', 'synthetic biology', or 'SynBio', 'brings together engineering and the life sciences in order to design and construct new biological parts, devices and systems that do not currently exist in the natural world or to tweak the designs of existing biological systems' (ETC Group, n.d.). Therefore, synthetic biology was brought into the CBD process out of necessity, out of concern, and out of interest. Environmental NGOs and IPOs have raised concerns about the potential impacts of biotechnology. Likewise, particular scientists, governments, and corporations have had an interest in the potential regulation of biotechnology and thus have been invested in the outcome of the negotiations surrounding these issues. Biotechnology is marked by intense scientific research, convoluted legal claims, and fast-paced advancements—all factors that confound the politicised, bureaucratic, and convoluted process of negotiating policy under the CBD. Additionally, as neoliberalism has impacted the global economy in promoting privatisation and eschewing the 'precautionary principle', the negotiations under the CBD that have been forced to take up issues associated with biotechnology often pit members of civil society against governments and industry in terms of their competing interests.

Patents at the intersection of science and law

On 13 June 2013, the Supreme Court of the United States reached a ruling on the patenting of naturally occurring human DNA. The case, *Association for Molecular Pathology* v. *Myriad Genetics, Inc.*, questioned the legality of Myriad's patents on the human genome sequences for BRCA1 and BRCA2, which have been associated with breast cancer. Women who seek testing to identify whether they are more at risk for certain types of breast cancer face often prohibitive costs as a result of Myriad's claims to patent rights. The court ruled unanimously that 'naturally occurring human DNA' could not be patented as it does not meet the criteria established under patent law. This decision served to overturn three decades of patents—the first human gene patent was awarded in 1982 to the University of California. Since then, the legality and ethics of owning rights to human gene sequences has been a highly contentious topic. By the time *Association for Molecular Pathology* v. *Myriad Genetics, Inc.* reached the Supreme Court, approximately 20 per cent of human genes had been patented. Many of those patents were filed by corporations, but approximately 30 per cent were filed by universities and other research institutions (many of which are funded by corporations). While the US Supreme Court determined that 'naturally occurring' human genes could not be patented, the justices argued that 'complementary DNA', or cDNA, *could* legally be patented. This distinguishes between human genes that have the same sequences that are found in cells and those sequences that are generated synthetically. This was a significant ruling with far-reaching ramifications, potentially for non-human genetic material. However, Austen Heinz, CEO of Cambrian Genomics, argued that this may be a moot point, as synthetic gene patents may become obsolete due to the fact that the bureaucratic patent process cannot keep pace with the massive innovations in industry and research. This represents a clear disjuncture between the world of science and technology and the world of policy-making, as participants within the context of the CBD have been faced with debating the possible regulatory challenges associated with biotechnology.

The precautionary principle

An exhaustive treatment of 'the precautionary principle' is not feasible in this particular context, as there is a wide body of scholarship on the subject (see, for example, Colombo and Steele 2016; Dickson and Cooney 2005), including a critique of how the principle can be counterproductive in the context of the MEAs within which it is found (Goklany 2001). However, as my focus here is on the ways in which particular tenets are deployed by participants as they strategically attempt to influence policy, it is important for readers to understand the intent of the precautionary principle and its centrality to the CBD. In the context of discussions that emerged around biotechnology, the precautionary principle has been an important element of the CBD lexicon for many participants. Essentially, the precautionary principle refers to the premise that, prior to engaging in any activity, one must ensure that there will be no adverse consequences of that activity. While that seems somewhat straightforward, in reality it becomes apparent that, like the very concept of 'biodiversity', what it means to apply the precautionary principle is quite complex. As debates under the CBD emerged around synthetic biology and biotechnology, for example, it is clear that participants in the negotiations have had differing senses of how to ascertain what the potential consequences of various activities would be. This has manifested itself in protracted debates not only about the deployment of new technologies but even about research related to those technologies, as will be discussed later in the chapter.

CBD COP10: Defining the conflict

In October 2010, the tenth Conference of Parties (COP10) to the CBD negotiated texts associated with the relevance of biotechnology to biological diversity. While multiple other issues were also on the agenda at this meeting, the negotiations surrounding biotechnology became contentious due to their implications for trade, intellectual property, and the potential for unintended consequences. The transformations related to how it is that biotechnology is being taken up under the CBD influence a multitude of current and ongoing policy-making processes. Here, with the goal of explicating larger questions related to current dynamics associated with global environmental governance, I analyse the work of practitioners in textually mediated processes associated with CBD policy negotiations. I focus on the perspective of CSOs as they engaged in (and responded to) the deliberations as their concerns and critiques provide opportunities for cutting through the policy language and exploring some of the larger philosophical, ethical, and ideological issues that are always present beneath the surface of the negotiating texts.

'Ethnographic snippet': CBD COP10

It's the first day of the tenth meeting of the COP to the CBD. I find my way to the meeting venue, partly by following the directions on the map of Nagoya, Japan, that I have, and partly, as I exit the subway station, by following the groups of people who are clearly COP participants. In any country, at any COP, we're a recognisable group comprised of clusters of individuals on the same government delegation discussing policy issues and members of civil society in less professional attire, yet equally concerned with being up to date on the status of the negotiations. Upon approaching the actual meeting site, UN security guards direct us to the entrance tent, where we show our identification and credential paperwork. The CBD has a photo of me on file from prior meeting attendance, so the printing of the badge is fairly *pro forma*. As with other CBD meetings, but unlike my credentials for meetings of other UN bodies that I attend, here I'm accredited as a non-governmental participant under the subheading of 'Education', as my university is able to supply the credentials.

I go through the security line, again thinking how similar this all is to going through airport security. Thankfully, I recall the Japanese word for 'empty' as I point to my metal water bottle. The Japanese security staff person smiles and nods, perhaps at my terrible pronunciation or perhaps at my attempts at speaking Japanese, a language that my 40-year-old brain has been struggling to learn for several months now. In Japan, I am regularly struck by how little I have to show for those efforts but nonetheless pat myself on the back every time I recognise a character or manage to successfully communicate in some extremely basic and mangled way. Here at the UN meetings, knowledge of Japanese is largely irrelevant. As with all other UN meetings I've attended around the globe, English is primary—and, with the exception of a few indicators of location represented in the host country's choice of logo or other showcased items, we could truly be almost anywhere. My knowledge of how UN meetings work is far more applicable than any knowledge of host-country language, as I orient myself to the scrolling list of events on the ubiquitous screens upon entering the campus of meeting rooms, Plenary halls, exhibition booths, postal services, and restaurants.

I've been following the CBD issues fairly intensively for about a year now, after having attended the 'CBD COP10 Preparatory Symposium' organised by the International Union for the Conservation of Nature and held in Tokyo, Japan on 6 September 2009 as I was conducting research on civil society participation in UN policy-making here in Japan. I subsequently attended the 'CBD Kobe Biodiversity dialogue' from 15–16 October 2009, in Kobe, Japan. Neither of these meetings was designed to negotiate policy, yet they highlighted some of the key dynamics that COP10 would address and served as part of Japan's lead-up to the actual COP—a COP that marked several milestones for the CBD and therefore held significant importance for Japan as the host country.

Prior to attending COP10 in Nagoya, I had attended meetings of the Ad-Hoc Working Group on Article 8(j) (AWG-8[j]) and the Working Group on Access and Benefit-Sharing (ABS) in Montreal in early November 2009. It was there that it became clear that dynamics associated with synthetic biology (or biotechnology) were clearly on the radar of environmental NGOs and IPOs. Many of the concerns that were raised by these participants involved what they saw as a disconnect between the interests of governments and the precautionary principle (or precautionary approach) (Peel 2004) that is a central element of the Convention itself.

Typically, my first couple of days at COPs and other major UN meetings tend to be marked by somewhat scattered wandering, as I use my best judgement to locate events that will be most useful for the threads of the processes I am trying to follow. Often, as I attempt to assess which negotiations are 'open' (accessible to 'observers' rather than just governments that are Parties to the Convention), I see a familiar face—someone I can ask about where and when particular negotiations will be held, or someone I can query about the current status of a particular agenda item. 'What is holding up the negotiations on ABS?' 'Do you know why Brazil took that position in Plenary yesterday?' 'Why would Colombia support that? I thought they were taking a different position on that issue under the UNFCCC.'

As an academic rather than a full-time policy participant, my paying job pulls me in a variety of directions away from the policy world. While I've spent extensive time in UN meetings over the past 20 years since I first entered the Palais des Nations in Geneva as a graduate student planning to conduct dissertation research on the Intergovernmental

Forum on Forests (IFF), my engagement in policy work—my research on UN environmental negotiations—has been contingent on both funding and time—both of which seem to be in incredibly short supply. The windfall of a fellowship from the Social Science Research Council greatly facilitated my ability to engage in a far more robust way between 2009 and 2011; however, I still feel somewhat like an interloper, as I can't help but feel as though anything but constant immersion in this world results in being generally clueless about the current state of affairs.

Amid the scrolling listings of meetings, I see a 'side event' hosted by the ETC Group called 'Synthetic Biology and Next Generation Biofuels' to be held in between larger Plenary sessions at 1.15 p.m. It is at side events organised by non-governmental and Indigenous groups and at the morning NGO briefing meetings that I learn the most about the various policy processes. Negotiations themselves are bogged down by tedious text-based deliberations or highly general statements reiterating governments' positions. Alternately, side events can provide the opportunity for frank discussions of issues of concern to particular participants. Participants' designated meetings, typically open only to those who are accredited through a particular category of participation (such as NGOs or the African Group, for example), also provide for the space for clear explanations of the status of negotiations. The NGO meetings that regularly took place over the course of COP10, typically in the morning before formal negotiations began, were designed to allow participants to report to each other on various agenda items so that other participants could be kept apprised of the various elements of the negotiations. Not only was it physically impossible for one person to be present in all simultaneous deliberations, but some discussions were closed to non-governmental participants, particularly as negotiations became more contentious.

As I proceeded to attend side events and NGO briefings at COP10, it became glaringly obvious that there were strong concerns about the way that the negotiations related to synthetic biology were headed. In the introduction to the side event 'Synthetic Biology and Next Generation Biofuels', it was noted that 'coming from SBSTTA14, two draft decisions tackle synthetic biology' (field notes, 18 October 2010). These draft decisions, which were being addressed by negotiators at COP10, fell under the agenda items of 'New and Emerging Issues' (Agenda Item 4.3 [e]) and 'Biofuels and Biodiversity' (Agenda Item 6.4). In further researching these documents, I noted that the entire text related to synthetic biology under 'New and Emerging Issues' (one paragraph) was in brackets, meaning governments had not come to an agreement on that paragraph during the course of SBSTTA14 and that much of the text related to 'Biofuels and Biodiversity' (comprising four pages, eighteen paragraphs, multiple sub-paragraphs, and multiple options) was in brackets, signifying that it was not only CSOs and IPOs who had issues with synthetic biology.

However, while the agenda items related to this topic were clearly identified, the fact that each was going to be addressed under a different Working Group presented problems for me as a researcher. 'Working Group I' was to be taking up 'New and Emerging Issues', whereas 'Biofuels and Biodiversity' fell under the work programme for Working Group II. Often at meetings where text negotiations take place, the Secretariat separates agenda items for work in concurrent meetings so that the entire agenda can reasonably be addressed by the end of the negotiations. This presents some problems for small delegations who feel the need to be multiple places at once. Compounding this issue at COP10 was the fact that negotiations on ABS were being held concurrently with the Working Groups. ABS had garnered enough attention to merit its own meetings which took place between COPs, much like the working Group on Article 8(j) (WG-8[j]). Some of the sticking points for the ABS had been related to access to—and the sharing of benefits from—genetic resources. Therefore, my decision to focus on the discussions surrounding genetics became somewhat problematic, given the fact that several meetings were often taking place simultaneously. I therefore decided to make Agenda Item 6.4—Biofuels and Biodiversity—my first priority and to garner as much information as possible about the other issues from side events, morning NGO meetings, and as many of the actual deliberations as I could attend. For the purposes of this analysis, I focus on the debates surrounding 'Biofuels and Biodiversity', as these deliberations provided fascinating windows into the competing interests of governments, corporations, CSOs, and IPOs.

Why biofuels? Government, corporate and CSO/IPO interests

Increasingly, nations are exploring options for reducing energy produced through the use of fossil fuels. In some cases, such as with the European Union, use of biofuels has been legislated as a means of reducing use of fossil fuel. This has provided a very substantial market for agriculture corporations. At the ETC Group side event, a presenter noted that Brazil was cultivating 8.8 million hectares of sugar cane. It was also noted that, at CBD COP9, Brazil had argued that the precautionary approach should not apply to biofuel production and that this was a non-negotiable position for the Brazilian delegation. Furthermore, Brazil was planning to release a genetically modified sugar cane in 2015 (field notes, 18 October 2010). It became clear that concerns about genetic modification were front and centre for CSOs and IPOs, yet, over the course of COP10, I heard additional concerns being raised related to biofuels. At several side events and morning NGO meetings, participants voiced concerns about the 'global land grab' that was currently taking place, whereby nation-states, in conjunction with large agricultural corporations, were either denuding natural forests to plant crops to be used for biofuels, or transforming existing cropland from food crops to biofuels. In the case of deforestation for biofuels, a clear intersection between the CBD and other bodies addressing land-tenure issues related to Indigenous Peoples emerged. In terms of replacing food crops with biofuels, CSOs and IPOs raised concerns related to the increasing costs of food as a result of the commodification of crops such as soy and corn as they are marketed for a growing biofuel economy. Clearly, CSO and IPO concerns were not unfounded. In an article by Macedo et al. published in 2012, the authors note that 'Global markets for commodities such as oil palm and soybeans are increasingly replacing local demand as the primary driver of tropical forest conversion for agriculture' (2012: 1341). They go on to emphasise that 'as global demand for food, fiber, and biofuels grows to unprecedented levels, the supply of available land continues to shrink ... fueling debate about how to reconcile the need for agricultural production with forest conservation and maintenance of ecosystem services such as carbon storage, climate regulation, and biodiversity conservation' (2012: 1341). While this research was yet unpublished at the time of COP10, CSOs and IPOs were well aware of these dynamics. Civil society groups' opening statements to COP10 reflected the fact that these issues were important to them. One of the points made by civil society during an intervention at the opening session of COP10 was that governments should 'halt the expansion of destructive industrial agriculture and aquaculture, bioenergy, biomass and other commodities' and that Parties (to the Convention) 'must adopt and uphold moratoria on the development, testing, release and use of new technologies which pose potential threats to biodiversity, including geoengineering and synthetic biology' (field notes, 18 October 2010). At one of the morning briefing meetings, NGOs noted that 'someone from Syngenta' was actually on the Brazilian delegation. Brazil made the case for this confluence of government and corporate interests based on the fact that people in the industry would understand the current state of the science related to synthetic biology as well as its intersections with patent law. All of these concerns played themselves out in the deliberations related to 'Biofuels and Biodiversity' over the course of the COP10 negotiations. As predicted, science has continued

to develop, creating new challenges for those involved in the negotiations, as I will address later in the chapter.

Texts as evidence of contentious debates

Throughout this book I have analysed the positions taken by various
participants in negotiations and have often referred to the fact that
many participants are invested in particular language associated with
the texts being negotiated. Participants engage with texts primarily by
making interventions in the context of plenaries or Working Groups.
However, Chairs and Co-Chairs also have a fair bit of influence over
which elements to include in subsequent drafts. Here I use actual texts
to represent the sort of work that negotiators engage in as they deliberate policy over the course of a given meeting. Not all iterations of this
particular text are included in this discussion, nor do I discuss the specific interventions made by governments as the texts transformed. This
would require far more space than exists in this manuscript, and, while
I attempted to document governments' interventions as I observed the
negotiations, the speed of the interventions outpaced my ability to fully
capture the sequence of interventions along with the complete substance of those interventions. However, the documents I have selected
to reproduce in the figures below give readers a sense of the discourse of
policy as well as the transformations in text. In addition, I address some
of the dynamics that were highly politicised during these particular
negotiations.

The first page of the original text coming from SBSTTA14 to COP10
is reproduced in Figure 4.1 (UNEP/CBD/COP10/1/Add.2/Rev.1). This
is the text that was used to initiate the deliberations on Agenda Item 6.4
('Biofuels and Biodiversity') at COP10.

The document, coming in to the COP10 deliberations, clearly outlines
the documentary precedent ('decision IX/2 of the Conference of
Parties', meaning that the second 'decision' of COP9 related to this particular agenda item) yet is also heavily bracketed, representing disagreement by governments about the language in the text. Of this four-page
document, Figure 4.2 represents the segment of the SBSTTA14 decision that directly addresses synthetic biology, represented in paragraphs
14 and 16. Notably, not only are these two paragraphs bracketed, but
paragraphs 15 and 18 are also in square brackets, representing the
fact that governments could not reach an agreement on the language
contained in those paragraphs at SBSTTA14. Throughout the entire
document, most references to 'land security' and 'indigenous and local
communities' remain bracketed, signifying contention over language

Item 6.4.   *Biofuels and biodiversity*

The following draft decision is taken from recommendation XIV/10 B of the fourteenth meeting of the Subsidiary Body on Scientific, Technical and Technological Advice (UNEP/CBD/COP/10/3).

The Conference of the Parties,

Recalling decision IX/2 of the Conference of the Parties;

[*Recognizing* that given the scientific uncertainty that exists, and the recent information that has emerged, significant concern surrounds the potential intended and unintended impacts of biofuels on biodiversity and impacts on biodiversity that would affect socio-economic conditions and food and energy security resulting from the production and use of biofuels [as well as impacts on land security] and on indigenous and local communities;]

[*Also recognizing* that improved monitoring, scientific assessment, open and transparent consultation, with the full and effective participation of indigenous and local communities, and information flow are crucial needs for the continuing improvement of policy guidance, and decision making, to promote the positive and minimize or avoid the negative impacts of biofuels on biodiversity and impacts on biodiversity that would affect socio-economic conditions and food and energy security resulting from the production and use of biofuels [as well as impacts on land security];]

1.   *Expresses its gratitude* to the European Union for its financial contribution towards the regional workshops for Latin America and the Caribbean, and Asia and the Pacific, and to the Government of Germany for the regional workshop for Africa, on ways and means to promote the positive and minimize the negative impacts of biofuel production and use on biodiversity, to the Governments of Brazil, Thailand and Ghana for hosting these workshops and to the Government of Brazil for providing Spanish interpretation to facilitate active participation of the entire region;

2.   *Invites* Parties, other Governments and relevant organizations and stakeholders to examine, and as appropriate, to further develop, based on scientific assessments on the impacts of biofuel production and use, and with the full and effective participation of indigenous and local communities, voluntary conceptual frameworks for ways and means to minimize or avoid the negative impacts and maximize the positive impacts of biofuel production and use developed by the three regional workshops; in further developing such voluntary conceptual frameworks, an effort should be made to focus the framework on the impacts of biofuel on biodiversity, and impacts on biodiversity that would affect socio-economic conditions and food and energy security resulting from the production and use of biofuels, as decided by the ninth meeting of the Convention of the Parties in decision IX/2;

[3.   *Urges* Parties and other Governments, in collaboration with indigenous and local communities and relevant organizations, when carrying out scientific assessments of the impacts of biofuel production and use to ensure that land rights, as appropriate and subject to national legislation [and applicable to international obligations], as well as the sustainable agricultural practices and food security of indigenous and local communities, are respected and promoted, and that steps are taken to redress any negative impacts on these communities by the production and use of biofuels;]

4.

Option A
[*Requests* the Executive Secretary, subject to the availability of financial resources, to:

(a)   Compile [and analyse] information on tools [and develop a toolkit] for voluntary use consisting of available standards and methodologies to assess direct and indirect effects and impacts on

/...

Figure 4.1 UNEP/CBD/COP/10/1/Add.2/Rev.1 (p. 160).
Reprinted with permission of the United Nations.

sustainable production and use of biofuels including land-use and water policies that promote the positive and minimize or avoid the negative impacts on biological diversity and impacts on biodiversity that would affect socio-economic conditions and food and energy security resulting from the production and use of biofuels, and to perform their impacts assessments of biofuel production and use at the national level;]

13. *Encourages* Parties and other Governments to develop and use environmentally-sound technologies, and support the development of research programmes and undertake impact assessments, which promote the positive and minimise or avoid the negative impacts of biofuel production and use on biodiversity and impacts on biodiversity that would affect socio-economic conditions and food and energy security resulting from the production and use of biofuels [as well as impacts on land security];

[14. *Decides to* convene an ad-hoc technical expert group on synthetic biotechnologies and other new technologies that are used or projected to be used in the next generation of biofuels to assess their impacts on biodiversity and related livelihoods.][55]

[15. *Invites* Parties, other Governments and relevant organizations to address both direct and indirect impacts that the production and use of biofuels might have on biodiversity, in particular inland waters biodiversity, on the services they provide and on indigenous and local communities;]

[16. *Urges* Parties and other Governments, in accordance with the precautionary approach, to ensure that living organisms produced by synthetic biology are not released into the environment until there is an adequate scientific basis on which to justify such activities and due consideration of the associated risks for the environment and biodiversity, and the associated socio-economic risks, are considered.]

17. *Recalling* decision IX/2 paragraph 3 (c)(i) of the Conference of the Parties, the precautionary approach should be applied to the production and use of biofuels in accordance with the preamble of the Convention on Biological Diversity;

18.

Option 1

[Recognizing the threats to biodiversity from the use of invasive alien species in biofuels production and use; *urges* Parties and other Governments to apply the precautionary approach following the guiding principles on invasive alien species contained in the Annex to decision VI/23[56];]

Option 2

[Recognizing the threats to biodiversity if species used in biofuel production become invasive; *urges* Parties and other Governments to apply the precautionary approach following the guiding principles on invasive alien species contained in the annex to decision VI/23[57];]

---

[55] This paragraph is in square brackets due to (i) financial implications, and (ii) a lack of consensus from the meeting on the need for the ad-hoc technical expert group and its mandate.

[56] One representative entered a formal objection during the process leading to the adoption of this decision and underlined that he did not believe that the Conference of the Parties could legitimately adopt a motion or a text with a formal objection in place. A few representatives expressed reservations regarding the procedure leading to the adoption of this decision (see UNEP/CBD/COP/6/20, paras. 294-324).

/....

Figure 4.2 UNEP/CBD/COP/10/1/Add.2/Rev.1 (p. 163). Reprinted with permission of the United Nations.

associated with those topics as well. Notably, during one of the negotiating sessions, Brazil objected to the use of the phrase 'land tenure
security', arguing that there was 'no international definition' of the
term. Here we see the importance of prior negotiations, including those
taking place in other fora, as the 'international definition' of terms gets
built up over time to become 'agreed-upon language' that can be used
in later deliberations. Another example of this dynamic involves the terminology that is used in this document pertaining to Indigenous Peoples.
At the time of COP10, several governments still had strong objections
to the term 'indigenous peoples' and advocated for the Convention language of 'indigenous and local communities'. The significance here is
that 'peoples', in international negotiations, had acquired meaning that
associated the term with sovereignty and self-determination, whereas
'communities' are simply groups of people living in a particular area
with varying forms of governance. As a result of the insistence of IPOs
and CSOs, and the lobbying of sympathetic governments, the current
(2018) terminology that is used under the CBD is 'indigenous peoples
and local communities', representing a seemingly small change in the
language yet a significant transformation in the meaning.

Also notable in Figures 4.1 and 4.2 is the bracketed text related to
science and biofuels. For CSOs and IPOs, as was evidenced in multiple side events, the possible 'unintended consequences' and 'scientific
uncertainty' that are referenced in the first preambular paragraph of the
SBSTTA14 document (see Fig. 4.1) were primary concerns. This is a
point of contention that has been a significant part of the debate about
genetically modified organisms (GMOs) since the ability to modify DNA
in laboratory settings has existed. Indeed, the 'precautionary principle'
signals a clear recognition that the changes that humans make to the
genetic structures of organisms could have unintended consequences
when those organisms are released into ecosystems within which they
did not naturally evolve. That these organisms could become 'invasive
alien species', as is referenced in paragraph 18 (both options) of the
SBSTTA14 text, was a major concern. That this text is bracketed, as is
the text calling for 'an ad-hoc technical expert group on synthetic biotechnologies and other new technologies' (paragraph 14), and the text
urging 'Parties and other governments, in accordance with the precautionary approach, to ensure that living organisms produced by synthetic
biology are not released into the environment until there is adequate scientific basis on which to justify such activities' (paragraph 16), signifies
considerable disagreement among governments regarding the potential
regulatory implications of a resulting COP decision.

As the negotiations on this agenda item proceeded, governments began to take increasingly polarised positions, with Brazil, Canada, Colombia, the EU, and New Zealand being identified by NGOs as coalescing on weakening the language associated with problematising biofuels, and Switzerland, the Philippines, and countries in the Africa Group pushing for stronger language on regulating biofuels. In fact, at one point, the Africa Group, upon seeing a 'Co-Chairs paper' that became available on Saturday, 23 October 2010, refused to continue to engage in negotiations. Not only were their prior suggestions not represented in the new text, but the very title of the document had been changed from 'Biofuels and Biodiversity' to 'Sustainable Biofuel Production and Use'. CSOs and IPOs became irate at this shift, arguing that the Co-Chairs were clearly biased towards the efforts to minimise the regulatory framework associated the production of biofuels. Figure 4.3 represents the first page of this contentious document, including notes that I made as the deliberations proceeded. These notes represent my efforts to capture the interventions on the text in real time. Typically, I entered negotiating sessions with several copies of the same document in order to have enough room in the margins to mark up the documents, as the Co-Chairs' successive drafts may indicate that certain segments need to be bracketed, yet they do not attribute that request to particular Parties.

The Co-Chair's paper that was intended to be the new negotiating text drastically alters the language around biofuels and even softens the concerns associated with land tenure and land security. In paragraph 1.bis (see Fig. 4.3), 'the security of land tenure' is to be addressed only 'where relevant for the implementation of the CBD', and, separated by a semicolon, the implications of this are to be noted 'in particular … for indigenous and local communities'. The wordsmithing of this paragraph relegates land-tenure security to cases that are relevant to the implementation of the CBD (which is quite vague) and relegates 'indigenous and local communities' to entities that appear to be a grammatical afterthought.

More distressing for governments who were opposed to this new text and for CSOs and IPOs was the fact that the new text reads as a far more uncritical acceptance of biofuels—not only as its title 'Sustainable Biofuel Production and Use' implies that the policy is now in support of biofuels and designed to organise sustainable production and use, but throughout the text references to 'scientific uncertainty' are downplayed or eliminated. As my notes in the margin indicate (see Fig. 4.3), the Philippines intervened to argue that the four new paragraphs (in the preamble) were actually inconsistent with some of the provisions

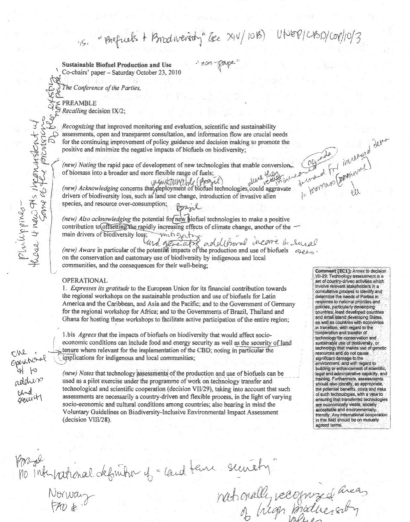

Figure 4.3 CBD COP10 'Co-Chair's Draft', Saturday, 23 October 2010. Reprinted with permission of the United Nations.

in the prior text that was being negotiated. In spite of this and other objections by governments who did not support this new text, other governments attempted to further weaken the existing language. As governments addressed the second 'new' paragraph, Brazil intervened to ask that the word 'unsustainable' be inserted, so that the sentence would read: '*Acknowledging* concerns that unsustainable deployment of biofuel technologies could aggravate drivers of biodiversity loss …'. This undermined the concerns of CSOs, IPOs, and governments, such as the Philippines. The Philippines intervened to reference its experiences with genetically modified crops, even referencing their history of colonisation and corporate control of their land, and argued that the new text did not contain language that captured their concerns.

Figure 4.4 represents the level of contention that existed on this agenda item, as the date and time changes at the top of the document indicate reworking of the document based on interventions by governments within the context of working-group sessions.

Figure 4.5 contains the paragraphs that were also represented in Figure 4.2, demonstrating how these paragraphs were being contested over the course of the negotiations spanning the majority of the two weeks of the meetings.

> Formatted: Font: 14 pt

NON-PAPER
13:pm, 26 October 2010

> Formatted: Font: 14 pt
> Formatted: Font: 14 pt
> Formatted: Font: 14 pt
> Formatted: Font: 14 pt

[TITLE TO READ: Agriculture and biodiversity: Consideration of ways and means to promote the positive and minimize the negative impacts of the production and use of biofuels on biodiversity]:

> Formatted: Font: 14 pt

The Conference of the Parties,

> Formatted: Font: 14 pt

Recalling decision IX/2 of the Conference of the Parties;

> Formatted: Font: 14 pt
> Formatted: Font: 14 pt
> Formatted: Font: 14 pt

PREAMBLE

> Formatted: Font: 14 pt
> Formatted: Font: 14 pt
> Formatted: Font: 14 pt

[*Recognizing* that the recommendations of the decisions on agricultural biodiversity also apply to the production of biofuels feedstocks to biofuels;]

> Formatted: Font: 14 pt

[*Recognizing* that continuing scientific uncertainty and concern exists in regard to given the scientific uncertainty that exists, and the recent information that has emerged, significant concern surrounds the potential intended and unintended impacts of biofuels on biodiversity [and impacts on biodiversity, that would affect socio-economic conditions and food and energy security resulting from the production and use of biofuels [as well as impacts on [land security][land-tenure security where they are relevant for the implementation of the CBD] and on indigenous and local communities;]
]

> Formatted: Font: 14 pt

[*Also rRecognizing* that-, improved research, monitoring and evaluation, scientific, socio-economic, and sustainability-scientific and environmental assessments, open and transparent consultation, with the full and effective participation of indigenous and local communities, and information flow are crucial needs for the continuing improvement of policy guidance, and decision making,- in order to address the uncertainties and concerns that exist regarding the potential intended and unintended impacts of biofuels on biodiversity and impacts on biodiversity that would affect related socio-economic conditions and to promote the positive and minimize or avoid the negative impacts of biofuels on biodiversity and the impacts on

> Formatted: Font: 14 pt

Figure 4.4 CBD COP10 'Non-Paper' on 'biofuels and biodiversity' (p. 1). Reprinted with permission of the United Nations.

18.

Option 1

[Recognizing the threats to biodiversity from the use of invasive alien species [used in agriculture including for] in biofuels feedstocks]production and use; *urges* Parties and other Governments to apply the precautionary principle approach following the guiding principles on invasive alien species contained in the Annex to decision VI/23[1];]

Option 2

[Recognizing the threats to biodiversity if species used in biofuel production become invasive or are known invasives; *urges* Parties and other Governments to apply the precautionary approach following the guiding principles on invasive alien species contained in the annex to decision VI/23[2]];

Recognising the threats [of existing or potentially invasive species] to biodiversity [if species used in biofuel production are [known to be or are potentially invasive] [potentially invasive, become invasive or are known to be invasive] or or if and to address the impacts of IAS already being used][of IAS used as biofuels crops] and for carbon sequestration, urges Parties and encourages other governments to [comply] apply the precautionary approach with regards to IAS following the guiding principles on IAS contained in the annex to decision VI/23[3]

Recognising the threats to biodiversity and the need to address the risks if species used in biofuel production become invasive or are known invasives or if IAS already being used [and for carbon sequestration], urges Parties and encourages other governments to apply the precautionary

Formatted: Font: 14 pt, Not Bold, Not All caps
Formatted: Font: 14 pt
Formatted: Font: 14 pt, Not Bold, Not All caps
Formatted: Font: 14 pt
Formatted: Font: 14 pt, Not Bold, Not All caps
Formatted: Font: 14 pt, Not Bold, Not All caps
Formatted: Font: 14 pt, Not Bold, Not All caps
Formatted: Font: 14 pt, Not Bold, Not Superscript/ Subscript, Not All caps
Formatted: Font: 14 pt
Formatted: Font: 14 pt, Not Bold, Not Superscript/ Subscript, Not All caps
Formatted: Font: 14 pt
Formatted: Font: 14 pt, Not Bold, Not Superscript/ Subscript, Not All caps
Formatted: Left
Formatted: Font: 14 pt, Not Bold, Not Superscript/ Subscript, Not All caps
Formatted: Font: 14 pt

---

[1] One representative entered a formal objection during the process leading to the adoption of this decision and underlined that he did not believe that the Conference of the Parties could legitimately adopt a motion or a text with a formal objection in place. A few representatives expressed reservations regarding the procedure leading to the adoption of this decision (see UNEP/CBD/COP/6/20, paras. 294-324).

[2] One representative entered a formal objection during the process leading to the adoption of this decision and underlined that he did not believe that the Conference of the Parties could legitimately adopt a motion or a text with a formal objection in place. A few representatives expressed reservations regarding the procedure leading to the adoption of this decision (see UNEP/CBD/COP/6/20, paras. 294-324).

[3] One representative entered a formal objection during the process leading to the adoption of this decision and underlined that he did not believe that the Conference of the Parties could legitimately adopt a motion or a text with a formal objection in place. A few representatives expressed reservations regarding the procedure leading to the adoption of this decision (see UNEP/CBD/COP/6/20, paras. 294-324)

Figure 4.5 CBD COP10 'Non-Paper' on 'biofuels and biodiversity', (p. 4). Reprinted with permission of the United Nations.

Finally, the 'non-paper' (represented in Figures 4.4 and 4.5) was turned into a CRP, that was then brought back to Plenary (from the Working Group) for governments to address.

Figures 4.6 and 4.7 represent the final documents that emerged as 'decisions' from COP10. The final text (decision X/37) has reverted to its original agenda item name ('Biofuels and Biodiversity'), representing the fact that enough governments had rejected transformations in that title.

However, the final text contains much of the language—and intent of that language—that existed in the Co-Chair's paper that was so contentious. The paragraph that acknowledges 'the potential for biofuel technologies to make a positive contribution to mitigating climate change' and that ties climate change to biodiversity loss (see Fig. 4.6) was seen

CBD

Convention on Biological Diversity

Distr.
GENERAL

UNEP/CBD/COP/DEC/X/37
29 October 2010

ORIGINAL: ENGLISH

CONFERENCE OF THE PARTIES TO THE
CONVENTION ON BIOLOGICAL DIVERSITY
Tenth meeting
Nagoya, Japan, 18-29 October 2010
Agenda item 6.4

DECISION ADOPTED BY THE CONFERENCE OF THE PARTIES TO THE CONVENTION ON BIOLOGICAL DIVERSITY AT ITS TENTH MEETING

X/37. Biofuels and biodiversity

The Conference of the Parties,

Recalling its decision IX/2, in which it decided to consider at its tenth meeting ways and means to promote the positive and minimize the negative impacts of the production and use of biofuels on biodiversity,

Recognizing that improved scientific, environmental and socio-economic research and assessments, open and transparent consultation, with the full and effective participation of the concerned indigenous and local communities, and sharing of best practices, are crucial needs for the continuing improvement of policy guidance and decision-making to promote the positive and minimize or avoid the negative impacts of biofuels on biodiversity and impacts on biodiversity that affect related socioeconomic conditions and to address the gaps in scientific knowledge and concerns that exist regarding such impacts,

Noting the rapid pace of development of new technologies that enable conversion of biomass into a broader and more flexible range of fuels,

Acknowledging concerns that deployment of biofuel technologies, may result in increased demand for biomass and aggravate drivers of biodiversity loss, such as land use change, introduction of invasive alien species, bearing in mind paragraph 6 of decision X/38 of the Conference of the Parties, and resource over-consumption,

Also acknowledging the potential for biofuel technologies to make a positive contribution to mitigating climate change, another of the main drivers of biodiversity loss, and generating additional income in rural areas,

Aware in particular of the potential positive and negative impacts of the production and use of biofuels on the conservation and customary use of biodiversity by indigenous and local communities, and the consequences for their well-being,

1.   *Expresses its gratitude* to the European Union for its financial contribution towards the regional workshops for Latin America and the Caribbean, and Asia and the Pacific, and to the Government of Germany for the regional workshop for Africa and to the Governments of Brazil, Thailand and Ghana for hosting these workshops to facilitate active participation of the entire region;

/...

Figure 4.6 CBD COP10 Decision X/37 (p. 1). Reprinted with permission of the United Nations.

15. *Encourages* Parties, in particular developed countries, and *invites* other Governments, financial institutions and other relevant organizations to provide technical and/or financial support to developing countries, in particular the least developed countries and small island developing States, as well as countries with economies in transition, to implement decision IX/2 and the current decision;

16. *Urges* Parties and other Governments to apply the precautionary approach in accordance with the Preamble to the Convention, and the Cartagena Protocol, to the introduction and use of living modified organisms for the production of biofuels as well as to the field release of synthetic life, cell, or genome into the environment, acknowledging the entitlement of Parties, in accordance with domestic legislation, to suspend the release of synthetic life, cell, or genome into the environment;

17. *Recognizes* that the consideration by the Subsidiary Body on Scientific, Technical and Technological Advice, in accordance with paragraph 4 of decision X/12, should assist in providing guidance and clarity on synthetic biology, and *encourages* Parties to include relevant information on synthetic biology and biofuels when submitting information in response to paragraph 4 of decision X/12.

Figure 4.7 CBD COP10 Decision X/37 (p. 3). Reprinted with permission of the United Nations.

as extremely problematic by CSOs and IPOs who have highlighted the inability for the climate regime to effectively address biological diversity, land tenure, and 'land grabbing'. Gone in this text is a reference to 'scientific uncertainty' that was previously in the SBSTTA14 preambular text (see Fig. 4.6). Paragraph 16 of the SBSTTA14 text (see Fig. 4.2), has been modified in the 'decision' document so that it, too, is absent of language that contains reference to scientific uncertainty. While 'the precautionary approach' is referenced, the clause referring to 'adequate scientific basis on which to justify' release of living modified organisms into the environment is no longer in the text.

Clearly, as the 'decision' document contains no brackets, all governments that had been negotiating the various iterations of the text over the two weeks of the meetings agreed to the final document. What is invisible in this text is the fact that governments understand that there must be 'consensus' texts at the end of the COP, and sometimes they concede on points that are important to them 'in the spirit of collaboration' or in order to be able to use that concession as a point of leverage in negotiations related to a different agenda item.

Subsequent negotiations: Keeping up with the science

Analysis of texts from meetings that followed COP10 indicate that biotechnology remains a contentious subject. Skipping ahead to the present (2018), current genetic modification that is being debated within the context of CBD negotiations and side events involves 'gene drive' technology. Essentially, the objective is to modify particular organisms with the express intent that the genetic modification will be 'driven' through the entire population. Examples of this sort of research involves genetically modifying mosquitoes so that they will no longer carry malaria, or modifying the DNA of rats to impact their fertility as a 'humane way to eliminate unwanted populations' (Hirschler 2017). Oye et al. argue that 'Potential beneficial uses of such "gene drives" include re-programming mosquito genomes to eliminate malaria, reversing the development of pesticide and herbicide resistance, and locally eradicating invasive species. However, drives may present environmental and security challenges as well as benefits' (2014: 626). These 'challenges' are clearly raising similar issues for CSOs and IPOs as biotechnology related to biofuel did nearly a decade ago. As Oye et al. noted, '[r]egulatory gaps must be filled before gene drives are used in the wild' (2014: 626). However, in 2018 there is still debate over whether those gaps have sufficiently been filled. This debate became evident at a side event for the SBSTTA22 meetings of the CBD on 3 July 2018, where scientists and academics on a panel seemed to believe that the potential for filling those gaps exists, whereas many attendees of the side event were clearly highly sceptical.

'Ethnographic snippet': CBD SBSTTA22

I've arrived at the side event just as it is about to begin and am frustrated to see that it has been scheduled to take place in a room that is far too small for the interest in the subject. Designed to fit a small group meeting, the room is not capable of holding the number of people who have arrived to attend the side event. Almost all of the available chairs are occupied, and multiple people are sitting on the floor, making entering the room a challenge. As I enter, someone who appears to be in charge of the event says to those of us clustered around the doorway, 'Come on in—there are a couple of chairs and some space on the floor.' I move towards the floor space he has indicated and notice a chair that is unoccupied. Taking care not to step on people on the floor, I ask the people near the chair if anyone is sitting there. They indicate that it is available, so I sit down. More people filter in and still several people are clustered at the doorway. There is considerable noise in the hallway outside the meeting room, as one of the side events has supplied lunch food to participants. The man who had previously taken charge raises his voice and suggests that we get started. One of the organisers introduces the side event and points out that there is someone filming a documentary (a man standing beside a large video camera on a tripod suddenly makes sense). The organiser states that anyone who is not interested in being filmed should indicate that fact, and not saying so would indicate consent. She then introduces the first panellist, who will be speaking on the regulatory framework for gene drives in Australia. He introduces himself and notes that, while he is speaking about this issue, he is not a regulator—his training is in entomology and ecosystem science.

As the various panellists speak, I note a disjuncture between the tone and content of the presentations and the substance of the questions that are posed to each panellist after they have concluded their talk. While the presenter who is discussing Australia's regulatory framework argues that part of his understanding of his organisation's mission is to 'not only question "Could we do this?", but also "Should we?"' (field notes, 3 July 2018), implying that the organisation is addressing the ethical questions associated with gene-drive technology, his ultimate conclusion seems to point in the direction of supporting an affirmative response to the question as to whether there are appropriate regulatory frameworks that could be put to use for gene-drive research. Significantly, he points out in his presentation that the literature that he has investigated along with his personal understanding of the regulatory framework available in Australia are both fairly consistent with the recommendations of the Chair's draft text and the 'discussion' that took place on 2 July as the relevant agenda item was being addressed in Plenary at SBSTTA22.

However, it becomes clear that not all participants in SBSTTA22 are on the same page regarding this agenda item. Fundamentally, what becomes apparent over the course of the panellists' presentations is that there is a general agreement among panellists that the 'precautionary principle' should be applied to all research associated with gene drives. While this is the language that is used in CBD negotiations, it does not seem to be sufficient to address the concerns of those in the audience. The majority of the questions posed by attendees speak to a broader concern about the use of gene-drive technology. This mirrors the disjuncture between policy-speak and the concerns of CSOs and IPOs that surface so often in these negotiations.

As I read through the texts in preparing for the meetings in Montreal, I was struck by the disconnect between the general tenor of the documents and the concerns about synthetic biology that I have heard being raised by NGOs since Nagoya. While the texts indicate that the precautionary principle should organise research related to gene drives, many CSOs are clearly concerned that there is no amount of precaution that would be sufficient to address the possible negative impacts of this technology. This was evident also in the back-and-forth between presenters and participants at the side event. At one point, a question was posed to a presenter who had just discussed the EU's approach to a potential regulatory framework for gene-drive research. 'Discussions of regulating gene-drive research are often related to both the nature of the organism and its receiving environment' began the attendee as he posed his question.

In the case of most gene-drive research, though, this becomes very problematic. For example, what is the nature of a mosquito? You will get change in the form of evolution so regulating that organism is impossible. Furthermore, what is the receiving environment? Mosquitoes don't stay in only one place. Since gene drives are designed to infiltrate a population, what are the boundaries of that population?

The presenter cut the participant off, as it seemed to be more of a statement than a question. 'Well, this is precisely the same critique that we heard about GMOs in the nineties', he began. 'Yes, and in fact that was legitimate—in Mexico, for example ...' responded the participant who had posed the question, beginning to engage in a direct debate with the presenter. My assumption is that he was going to reference the dynamics associated with GMO corn and the well-documented detriment to native strains of maize in Mexico. At this point, the presider put a halt to this debate and indicated that we needed to move on.

The following day, while the agenda items that were being addressed did not include synthetic biology, genetic sequencing or gene drives, a side event that took place after the official negotiations further highlighted the tensions that had emerged in the prior side event. Unlike the side event on 3 July, the presentations included in the 4 July side event were much more in line with the views of those posing the questions to the presenters the day prior. The title of the side event was 'Gene Drives: For Agricultural to Military Use—Ethics, Rights, Power, Science and Precaution'. One of the groups sponsoring the side event was the ETC Group, a group that had been highly active in discussions and side events in Nagoya at COP10.

Presenters took a far more critical approach to gene-drive technology, noting concerns that were similar to those raised in the questions posed to the panellists in the side event the day before. In fact, two of the panellists had actually raised critical questions in the prior side event. One of the presenters Skyped in from Burkina Faso, highlighting a lack of transparency between local communities and researchers working on gene-drive technology. After the presentations, the organiser of the side event asked for questions for the panellists, suggesting that Parties (government participants) be allowed to go first, as 'contact groups' were meeting that evening and she recognised that government negotiators would need to leave the room. One of the attendees, who identified herself as being on the delegation for Burkina Faso, rather than asking a question, indicated that she had a different experience with researchers than was articulated by the Skype presenter. The next attendee who posed a question identified himself as being on the Swiss delegation. He indicated that some of the panellists would remember debates over GMOs that took place during COP8 and asked the presenters what had changed. In his question, he referenced the fact that members of civil society were concerned that genetically modified trees would become invasive species and greatly disrupt ecosystems. In his view, this hadn't happened. What, he wondered, was different about gene drives? Were they simply rehashing an old debate?

The exchange that took place regarding this question was very instructive as to how various participants view the dynamics associated with biotechnology. In many ways, the panellists were hard pressed to identify what was *categorically* different about gene-drive research, although one of the presenters noted that gene drives are *intended* to modify entire populations, and they are *intended* to spread. However, this was expressed to be on the same continuum with other genetic modifications, as similar concerns were reiterated related to the lack of scientific evidence that the technology would not cause irreparable harm to ecosystems. For CSOs and IPOs, as was represented in the title of the side event, biotechnology is inherently tied in with other interests— interests which may present disjunctures between the policy texts and actually arrest the loss of biological diversity. CSOs and IPOs are very aware of the fact that all of the factors of 'ethics, rights, power, science and precaution', as the subtitle of the side event referenced, are wrapped up in biotechnology. Rather than seeing the UN as a place where strong policies designed to protect the environment and the livelihoods of marginalised peoples are fostered, CSOs and IPOs are justifiably critical of the outcomes of years of deliberations, as was demonstrated in the weakening of the text associated with 'Biofuels and Biodiversity' that took place over the course of COP10.

In the following (concluding) chapter, I return to this dynamic that threads throughout the book: the fact that many participants view the policy processes that take place under the auspices of UN-based environmental negotiations as being incapable of arresting the very environmental degradation they are designed to address. As the examples that were raised in this chapter illustrate, 'the environment' as it is negotiated, is never divorced from ethics, rights, power, and science.

References

Colombo, C. and K. Steele (2016) 'Philosophy and the Precautionary Principle: Science, Evidence, and Environmental Policy', *British Journal for the Philosophy of Science*, 67: 1195–2000.

Cutler, K.M. (2013a) 'Bio-Hackers, Get Ready', *Techcrunch*, available at http://techcrunch.com/2013/05/26/cambrian-genome-compiler/ (accessed 20 August 2013).

—— (2013b) 'Supreme Court Ruling on Gene Patenting May Be a Boon for Biotech Startups', *Techcrunch*, available at http://techcrunch.com/2013/06/17/supreme-court-ruling-on-gene-patenting-may-be-a-boon-for-biotech-startups/ (accessed 20 August 2013).

Dickson, B. and R. Cooney (2005) *Biodiversity and the Precautionary Principle: Risk and Uncertainty in Conservation and Sustainable Use*, London and Sterling, VA: Earthscan.

ETC Group (n.d.) *Synthetic Biology*, available at www.etcgroup.org/issues/synthetic-biology (accessed 18 December 2016).

Goklany, I.M. (2001) *The Precautionary Principle: A Critical Appraisal of Environment Risk Assessment*, Washington, DC: CATO.

Hirschler, B. (2017) 'Rats Join Mosquitoes as Targets for "Gene Drive" Pest Control', Reuters, Science News, 5 December, available at https://www.reuters.com/article/us-science-pests-genes/rats-join-mosquitoes-as-targets-for-gene-drive-pest-control-idUSKBN1DZ2GC (accessed 24 July 2018).

Intergovernmental Platform on Biodiversity and Ecosystem Services (IPBES) (n.d.) *About: What Is IPBES?* available at www.ipbes.net/about-ipbes.html (accessed 16 September 2016).

Oye, K.A., K. Esvelt, E. Appleton, F. Catteruccia, G. Church, T. Kuiken, S. Bar-Yam Lightfoot, J. McNamara, A. Smidler, and J.P. Collins (2014) 'Regulating Gene Drives', *Science*, 345(6197): 626–8.

Parthasarathy, S. (2011) 'Whose Knowledge? What Values? The Comparative Politics of Patenting Life Forms in the United States and Europe', *Policy Sciences*, 44(3): 267–88.

Peel, Jacqueline (2004) 'Precaution: A Matter of Principle, Approach or Process?' *Melbourne Journal of International Law*, 5(2): 483.

Takacs, D. (1996) *The Idea of Biodiversity: Philosophies of Paradise*, Baltimore, MD: Johns Hopkins University Press.

UNEP (1992) Convention on Biological Diversity, available at www.cbd.int/doc/legal/cbd-en.pdf (accessed 21 September 2018).

Wilson, E.O. (ed.) (1988) *Biodiversity*, Washington, DC: National Academy Press.

5   The elephant in the room

The treadmill of production as the root cause of environmental harm

'The closer you get to UN procedures, the farther you get from home'.
(Indigenous participant in the CBD COP10 meetings,
field notes, 19 October 2010)

'Let's be real. We need to address the elephant in the room', stated Maori activist Catherine Davis at a side event on the REDD programme held in conjunction with the annual meeting of the UNPFII. For Davis, the 'elephant in the room' was the global capitalist system that contributes to dynamics that are directly associated with deforestation and the marginalisation of Indigenous Peoples. Davis noted concerns that have been raised associated with REDD since its inception: that the commodification of land under REDD schemes serves not only to place a market value on natural forests but also to further jeopardise the land-tenure rights of Indigenous Peoples. Long et al. concur with this analysis and argue that 'the fate of the REDD negotiations reveals the domination of neo-liberal ideology within the UNFCCC, and the difficulty in articulating any mechanism for reducing carbon emissions within this space that does not also increase corporate power and expand the opportunities for market mechanisms' (2010: 225). Davis, as an Indigenous activist who has been engaged in broader debates about land tenure and environmental policy, was directly referring to the system of global capitalism that undergirds environmental degradation. Her usage of this particular idiom speaks volumes as she was very clear about pointing out the fact that there is an obvious connection between the current hegemonic system of growth-based capitalism and environmental degradation—yet, while this connection is as mammoth as an elephant in a room, most participants talk around it as if it were not there. This is partly by design as 'agenda items' do not reference consumption or production patterns, nor do they allow for treatment of economic systems.

However, it is here that the broader terrain of global governance has been subsumed under the taken-for-granted beneficence of the system of global capitalism to which many dominant nation-states subscribe.

As I have noted at various points throughout this book, opportunities to critique the connections between a broader global economy (that is predicated on a narrowly defined requirement of economic growth) and environmental degradation are scarce within UN environmental deliberations. I have made this case in further detail throughout this book by way of examples from the negotiations. While there are some opportunities for discussions of science (albeit enshrouded in myriad often conflicting interests), and deliberations are intended to get closer to developing policies that will address environmental problems, there are virtually no opportunities in policy processes for participants to inject references to *actual root causes* of environmental degradation such as those related to the current workings of the global economy. Even discussions of 'root causes' identify drivers of deforestation or loss of biodiversity as 'agriculture' or 'mining' but do not place these phenomena within the context of a global economic framework that organises *what sort* of agriculture (industrial), and *what sort* of mining (as an extractive industry). Discussions of 'root causes' do not address the taproot, which remains 'the elephant in the room', in Davis's terminology.

It is clear that the concept of 'sovereign rights to resources' is enshrined in UN agreements, as one can find reference to nations' sovereign rights to resource use in virtually every environmental policy negotiated within the context of the UN. However, I argue that the primary impediment to true environmental and social change taking place as a result of policies negotiated under the auspices of the UN is not sovereignty per se, but instead the incompatibility between nation-states' economic interests and positive social or environmental outcomes. Fundamentally, states are unwilling to abandon the dominant model that organises the current global economy—a model that ties economic growth to increasing production and consumption. This 'treadmill of production' (Schnaiberg 1980) stands in stark contrast to the purported goals of each of the UN bodies I observed. UN negotiations are destined to simply 'rearrange the deck chairs on the Titanic' as long as the current economic order remains unchallenged. This is not to say that these negotiations should be abandoned, or that nations have a right to withdraw from important agreements or bodies (such as the Paris Agreement or the Human Rights Council, for example), but the opportunities for arresting environmental degradation and the concomitant human-rights violations that accompany such degradation are minimised within a context of a broader system that holds nation-states hostage to particular economic models. In this concluding chapter, I explicitly address the fundamental impasse that prevents UN policy negotiations from achieving their stated goals, namely that the global economy is predicated on 'the treadmill of production' (Schnaiberg 1980), which requires production and consumption in the process of accumulating capital (Dauvergne 2008; Harvey 2014).

'Ethnographic snippet': Global expert workshop on REDD

Gathered around a rectangle of tables on the morning of 20 September 2010 were approximately sixty individuals who had come to the UN office in Nairobi for the 'Global Expert Workshop on Biodiversity Benefits of Reducing Emissions from Deforestation and Forest Degradation in Developing Countries' (hereafter referred to as 'the Expert Workshop') that had been organised by the CBD. Included in the participants were thirty-two individuals representing governments, five representing intergovernmental organisations, nine affiliated with the UN in various capacities, six representing ILCs, and eight of us categorised as 'others'—a group which was primarily comprised of individuals from environmental NGOs. As a researcher, I was an outlier in the group, as others attending the workshop had been directly engaged in various levels of policy negotiation, primarily under the auspices of the CBD.

Significantly, debates about REDD have emerged as a locus of concerns for environmental CSOs and IPOs regarding many of the issues that do not have direct correlations in agenda items in intergovernmental negotiations—namely, rights of marginalised people and the commodification of nature. Both of these issues are deeply interconnected as mechanisms of the current global economy (Eastwood 2011). The key issue for participants in the CBD is that the REDD framework emerged out of deliberations taking place under the UNFCCC. In this context, the goal was to develop a scheme whereby forests (primarily in the Global South) would be valued so that they would be more likely to be maintained. For the UNFCCC, REDD programmes were proposed as a solution to deforestation. Governments understood that GHG emissions were unlikely to be reduced and therefore needed to be absorbed. As forests operate as natural 'carbon sinks', the REDD discussions under the UNFCCC gained significant traction.

It was within this context that the Expert Workshop was convened from 20 to 23 September 2010 in Nairobi, Kenya. In opening the Expert Workshop, the representative from the CBD Secretariat made reference to the CBD COP9 Decision IX/5, which '[i]nvites Parties, other Governments and relevant international and other organisations to: (a) Ensure that possible actions for reducing emissions from deforestation and forest degradation do not run counter to the objectives of the CBD and the implementation of the programme of work on forest biodiversity'. A major point of contention for CSOs and IPOs who were participating in UNFCCC negotiations as REDD programme proposals were emerging was that the policy texts focused solely on forests as carbon-absorbing entities and not as complex entities that contributed to maintaining rich biological diversity. In fact, given the lack of specification of what counted as a 'forest' in the REDD policy debates, monoculture, non-native tree plantations could take the place of 'natural' forests and still be considered to be carbon sinks.

The CBD, in its Decision IX/5 (quoted above), also references the CBD 'programme of work on forest biodiversity' explicitly. The 'expanded programme of work on forest biological diversity' preceded REDD in that it was adopted at the sixth COP of the CBD in 2002. With twelve 'goals', twenty-seven 'objectives', and 130 'activities', the CBD's 'expanded programme of work on forest biological diversity' addresses a range of dynamics and serves to specify the importance of forests to biological diversity. At the Expert Workshop in Nairobi, we were given a copy of the 'Overview of the Expanded Programme of Work on Forest Biodiversity' as a means to orient participants to the relevance of forests to the work of the CBD.

It is not unusual for bodies associated with intergovernmental environmental policy deliberations to hold 'expert workshops'. All expert workshops are carefully crafted to address particular dynamics that are relevant to the policy terrain. However, what became clear to me over the days of the workshop, was that several participants were bringing concerns to the table that did not have concurrent agenda items. The careful crafting of the workshop program allowed for the CBD to make recommendations to the UNFCCC yet served to eliminate the space for particular discussions to legitimately take place. As participants attempted to interject concerns about the fundamental premise of REDD— that giving forests a market value will encourage their preservation— organisers of the workshop regularly moved the discussion back to the previously established agenda, an agenda that was very much consistent with existing language that exists under the CBD and UNFCCC.

To say that REDD has created significant controversy is an understatement. In fact, at *every* CBD, UNFCCC, UNPFII or UNFF meeting I have attended since 2010, I have gathered evidence of a sustained critique of REDD programmes as a solution to climate change. Whether in the form of flyers decrying the impact of REDD programmes on Indigenous Peoples' rights, or side events designed to call REDD programmes into question, each of the meetings I have attended associated with these bodies has contained some evidence of CSO and IPO critique. The basis of the criticism has primarily been predicated on concerns related to the impacts bringing natural forests under the logic of the market, which serves to encourage government or corporate control and further jeopardise access to resources and land-tenure security. A concurrent academic analysis of the UNFCCC negotiations supports this claim, arguing that 'the marketisation of the natural environment dominates as a "climate solution" within UN processes' (Long et al. 2010: 222). As a result of sustained criticism, primarily by IPOs and CSOs but also coming from other intergovernmental bodies such as the CBD, REDD programmes transformed to begin to incorporate 'safeguards'. Hence, the revision of REDD to become 'REDD+', a policy framework that was intended to reflect and respond to concerns. However, as Takacs notes, the actual ability for REDD+ programmes to address the original concerns remained unrealised.

> Despite its promised potential, critics claim that REDD+ does not mitigate global climate change, and instead violates human rights, circumvents democracy, is methodologically suspect and unworkable in practice, and allows the already rich (mostly in the global North) to profit at the expense of the poor (in the global South) they are allegedly aiding.
>
> (2014: 77–8)

Furthermore, Takacs suggests that 'REDD+ is a laboratory for reforming not just forest governance and management, but also governance and management of all environment development projects. ... So, for example, the UN-REDD Programme is investing many millions in REDD+ in forty-four nations' (2014: 123). These vast investments, and a sense of lack of control on the local level over these new governance frameworks, did not go unnoticed by participants in UNFCCC and CBD negotiations as the REDD (and subsequently REDD+) deliberations were being played out.

'Ethnographic snippet': Global civil society workshop on the Rio+20 'Zero Draft' and rights for sustainability

Now (24 January 2012) I'm in New York, attending a day-long workshop that is intended to get members of 'civil society' up to speed for the subsequent three days of negotiations (25–7 January 2012) that will be taking place within UN headquarters. Governments are engaging in a series of 'informal' discussions as they hash out the 'Zero Draft'— meaning the draft that is not yet numbered for actual deliberations— prior to the negotiations that will be taking place at Rio+20 at the UN Conference on Sustainable Development.

The informational packet for participants in the workshop contains a handout that is intended to orient us to the matters we'll be discussing over the course of the workshop. Referencing the Rio+20 negotiations that will be taking place, the handout points to the fact that, in the 20 years since the original UNCED in Rio (1992), '[g]lobal economic expansion continues to severely strain the environment' and, 'despite the vast amounts of wealth being produced, the benefits are shared very unequally, with the wealthiest 20 per cent of humankind enjoying over 70 per cent of total world income' (IBON 2012). Also included in the packet of informational papers was a 'policy brief' titled: 'Green Economy: Gain or Pain for the Earth's Poor' (Verzola and Quintos 2012). In this and other arenas where members of civil society discuss UN policy processes, the notion of a 'green economy' was one that many CSOs and IPOs took issue with, as they argued that it further entrenches a framework that serves to commodify nature. Many participants, over the course of the workshop, raised issues associated with this new UN rhetoric, arguing that it supplanted 'sustainable development' yet did not rectify the problems associated with the prior term. Instead, they argued that the global economic system was merely absorbing 'green' technologies and 'green' incentives rather than truly transforming in a way that could promote actual sustainable futures for marginalised people and for the environment itself.

At one point, one of the presenters at the workshop attempted to make suggestions for effective civil society involvement. 'The Zero Draft document is a hook on which to hang more ambitious language', he said. 'How well do you know the text?' he continued. 'How much of the language that you want is in the documents? Agreed language is often a panacea to turmoil in the negotiations.' When things get stuck, 'Then you just need to know your UN history. From where can we pick up more ambitious language? Go to these meetings [of the Zero Draft] and see if there is language here to strengthen your position.' Furthermore, in order to be most effective, he argued that participants should 'develop an enabling phrase or paragraph that fits into the correct area of the document. For example, you'll see that in paragraph 24 has the necessary basis for corporate social responsibility' (field notes, 24 January 2012). The advice that was being given was sound, in the sense that participants must 'work within the system' in order to be heard. However, many participants voiced concerns that 'the system' would not allow for a strengthening of 'language' that could encapsulate their world view. In the afternoon, during a session under the heading of 'Sumak Kawsay Principles and New Paradigms for Sustainability', this disjuncture between the world of UN process and alternate world views was clearly articulated. The presenter, from 'Oilwatch', took issue with the fact that the outcome document for Rio+20 was to be titled 'The Future We Want':

> The Andean Quechua concept of 'Kawsay' is meant to express what it means to 'live well', not just to be 'sustainable'—or to 'develop'. These are words that we do not understand. Who is this 'we' that they speak of? For Latin America, we need a *post*-development concept—not a sustainable development concept. We recognise that nature is a subject—a subject with rights. We are a state with different nationalities—a plurinational state—and different cultures have different ways of understanding rights. The green economy has been built and shaped and forged with the cartesian understanding that humans are positioned against nature. In the NGO statement, the only thing we can put to governments—we need to tell them that they need to redo the Zero Draft from the beginning—from *below* zero, because the only thing in that draft right now is a deepening of neoliberalism.

This scathing critique was then supported by the next presenter, from the Third World Network. 'The time to be critical is now', he said. 'The Green Economy Roadmap has served to make the private sector the key driver for the SDGs (Sustainable Development Goals)' (field notes, 24 January 2012).

As presenters and others participants engaged in the discussions throughout the workshop, it was clear to me that a very different arena had been established here, where talk of capitalism, neoliberalism, and problems with allowing the private sector to be the 'key driver' of policy processes was *not* marginal. This is the arena of CSO and IPO discussions, where the policy language that serves to obfuscate the issues at hand was criticised and the very process of negotiating texts under UN deliberations was recognised to be at odds with the future—and indeed the present—that these participants truly wanted. Demonstrating a keen sense of the negotiation process, yet refusing to accept the terms of the debate as those terms are established within the UN, the participants in the civil society workshop articulated a profound critique of what they saw as being the root problems of both environmental degradation and further marginalisation of marginalised people: the neoliberal global capitalist system. Significantly, they regularly predicated this critique on their real lived experiences with 'development'. This discussion caused me to recall the quotation that serves as an epigraph to this chapter: 'The closer you get to UN procedure, the farther you get from home.' This was stated by a member of an IPO during a side event in Nagoya at the CBD COP10 in 2010. She attributed this statement to have been made originally by an Indigenous chief, yet she argued that it rang true to her. Participants in the policy-making processes that take place under the auspices of the UN understand the dominant discourses, accepted rules of process, and very nature of the agenda items that are structured around an entire textual legacy are not compatible with their lived experiences 'on the ground'. They recognise that these procedures do not open up spaces for them to articulate their primary concerns and are thus relegated to the margins as 'members of civil society'. As Long et al. argue, 'these tensions are particularly acute in debates about how to engage with the UNFCCC process, and, what is increasingly part of the UNFCCC, the market-based mechanisms playing a role of increasing prominence in climate governance' (2010: 226). Clearly, as the multiple examples that have been presented in this book illustrate, this is relevant not only to the UNFCCC. The confluence of marketisation and environmental policy—or, more accurately, the subsuming of environmental policy under the primacy of market forces, creates an untenable contradiction.

Ethnographic snippet: UNPFII16 and UNPFII17

I'm back in New York, here to attend the sixteenth meeting of the UNPFII. The theme of this session of the Permanent Forum is 'Tenth Anniversary of the United Nations Declaration on the Rights of Indigenous Peoples: Measures Taken to Implement the Declaration'. Negotiations of the United Nations Declaration on the Rights of Indigenous Peoples (UNDRIP) itself took decades and were highly contentious. However, for a decade now, participants in a range of arenas can point to the Declaration as setting the bar for 'agreed-upon language' in an effort to move other processes forward.

I always look forward to attending meetings of the UNPFII. Not only is any meeting room filled with participants who represent marginalised people around the world, but the interventions and agenda items tend to allow people to cut through the typical UN diplomacy. As interventions are being made in a Plenary session, I'm aware of some activity that is taking place to my right. Typically conversations take place throughout the meetings, so a regular drone of background noise is to be expected.

However, this becomes an interruption. An individual, who is being filmed on a smartphone, is demanding that the meeting Chair allow for people to address the current crisis that is taking place at Standing Rock. Suddenly the meeting is in a state of semi-chaos, as most participants are so used to the typical modes of procedure that the disruptive actions take people by surprise. There seems to be a reluctance to stop the interruption, as the issues being raised resonate with many in the room and have been the topic of discussion in formal interventions, side events, and in the corridors at various points throughout the meeting. This has become such a point of discussion that I have actually started thinking about why it is that the injustices at Standing Rock have taken up disproportionate space here. My experience at previous UNPFII meetings has allowed me to fill my notebooks with first-hand accounts of horrifying evidence of repression against Indigenous Peoples around the world. And, indeed, I have been tuned in to the militarised response to the activists who are opposing the Dakota Access Pipeline at Standing Rock as various elements of that activism have been reported in the alternative press. I've been outraged that protesters at Standing Rock have been attacked by law-enforcement dogs, sprayed with water hoses in the sub-zero temperatures of the South Dakota winter, tear gassed, arrested, incarcerated … I have been following these protests, as I too have engaged in civil disobedience in opposition to the expanding fossil-fuel infrastructure, and I feel anger and dismay at the corporate, state, and federal response to the actions of the protesters at Standing Rock. Clearly, these individuals are attempting to intervene in the fossil-fuel infrastructure. The threat that these activists pose is not only to the expansion of fossil fuels. The true threat is related to the fact that the expanding fossil-fuel infrastructure is inextricably linked to the accumulation of capital.

Is the prominence of Standing Rock at UNPFII16 related to the fact that this struggle is taking place in the Global North, where the rights of citizenship are supposed to protect individuals against bodily harm? Of course this is the space where these issues need to be raised. But is there something else going on here? Has Standing Rock provided the space for people to recognise that the primacy of capital is now creating a new terrain for those in the Global North who once thought that the nation-state would stand on their side in opposition to the corporation?

Some of these questions were answered the following year at UNPFII17. As I attended a side event during which LaDonna Brave Bull Allard, the woman who allowed protesters to utilise her land to create the camp at Standing Rock, gave an impassioned recounting of the events. By the end of her story, during which she chronicled the injustices and abuses that she and the other protesters experienced, the majority of the attendees in the room were visibly moved, some of us to tears. She told of how the protesters had erected a fence to prevent the machinery that was intended to work on the pipeline from entering the sacred area:

> [S]o the fence went down, so then they [the protesters] tried to push those guys back because they were attacking women and children, and then all these dogs were out there, and I was just like—standing out there. And I was just standing out there among those dogs thinking, 'Where the heck *am* I? This is not *America* ... this is not what *I* thought it would be ...'. This woman was siccing a dog on people, and blood was running from its mouth, and it was a big grey—and I was just standing there, and I kept saying, 'This is not true!' And the young men came with their horses and got between us and the dogs—and the dogs started biting the horses, and I just kept thinking, 'Oh my God! What is happening here?' and the men started throwing their dogs in the vehicles, and they started leaving, so the people ran, and they went out there to where everything was dug up, and people cried, and prayed, and put tobacco down. Because there was nothing else we could do. And at that moment I thought, 'The law is not just.' I always understood that America was not just. I always thought that no matter what we could do, we could educate, we can do things better, we can be better people— and at that moment, I realised no. No.

Allard went on to recount more details of the events, highlighting the increasing surveillance of protesters and her understanding of the circumstance as being marked by the importance of wealth at the expense of people's well-being. Subsequent presenters at the side event cited the fact that over fifty-eight pieces of legislation that further criminalise activism related to fossil-fuel infrastructure have been introduced in the United States. Allard's recounting of the incidents and articulation of her loss of faith in law was telling. Clearly, as increased incidents of racism and backlashes against immigration have revealed inequalities in countries in the Global North that are at odds with the rhetoric of inclusion and equality of opportunity that many of these countries espouse. Indeed, even that rhetoric is currently under fire in the United States, where politics and racism can no longer be disentangled. As an Indigenous woman in the United States, Allard is well aware of the level of internal colonisation experienced by Native nations. However, her experiences at Standing Rock demonstrated to her in a very visceral way that humans are expendable and profit reigns supreme.

The treadmill produces environmental harm

The confluence of corporate and government objectives is not new, yet it has been gaining strength as neoliberalism increasingly impacts the workings of governments around the globe. McMichael (2012) quotes James Linen, then president of Time-Life, Inc., as opening a Time-Life, Inc. meeting between corporations, governments, and Indonesian coup leader General Suharto as stating:

> We are here to create a new climate in which private enterprise and developing countries work together ... for the greater profit of the free world. This world of international enterprise is more than governments ... .It is the seamless web of enterprise which has been shaping the global environment at revolutionary speed.
>
> (Linen, quoted in McMichael 2012: 113)

This confluence between corporations and governments, at the expense of actual democracy (as in the case of Indonesia), has been well documented. From the agricultural technologies that were foisted on the Global South in the name of 'development' and a discourse of 'feeding the world' through the Green Revolution, to military technologies that have likewise been marketed to the Global South, corporate/government influence has created a world that is marked by increasing polarity between wealth and poverty. Significantly, the global-development apparatus has long poised itself as addressing global poverty. However, the root causes of inequality are not addressed, as the panacea to the ills of poverty have been caged within a discourse that is consistent with neoliberal economic premises. McMichael addresses this dynamic as he analyses 'the refusal, or inability, of the development agencies ... to address global *inequality*, to refocus on how neoliberal development aids the rich more than—or at the expense of—the poor' (2012: 218–19, italics in the original). Pieterse articulates the discourse of development as being consistent with neoliberal logic in that 'the object of concern is not global inequality but global poverty, the instrument of analysis is economic data processing, and the bottom-line remedy is freeing up market forces, now with a human face' (2002: 1033).

These references merely scratch the surface of the wide body of scholarship that exists as a critical analysis of the global development apparatus and its strong commitment to a neoliberal economic paradigm. Social movements have emerged to contest the workings of the global economy, such as the infamous revolution in opposition to the privatisation of water in Bolivia in 1999–2000, and 'the battle of Seattle' in opposition to the WTO in 1999. Throughout the twenty-first century, mining, energy, and industrial agriculture projects have been met with sustained opposition from people on the ground in specific locations where these projects have an impact. Contesting this broader economic paradigm is dangerous, as participants in the UNPFII regularly cite the fact that more and more environmental activists are killed every year, and activists, such as those contesting the Dakota Access Pipeline at Standing Rock, are facing increased militarisation and criminalisation.

Based on the 20 years of participation in UN meetings that I have engaged in, it is becoming increasingly clear to me that CSOs and IPOs represent a crucial force in the deliberations, if only to bring the *actual* issues back into the debates. Governments are drawn into a range of dynamics in this shifting global economy and are jockeying for position in ways that serve to sideline the dynamics that the deliberations are intended to address. While the fate of the UN is unclear, it is evident that the underpinning of nation-states' positions is linked to the broader global economic system which serves to subsume environmental policy-making processes. As long as the dominant economic paradigm remains one that is narrowly based on the notion of infinite growth, it will be the role of CSOs and IPOs to problematise this dynamic, and to 'hold governments' feet to the fire'.

References

Dauvergne, P. (2008) *The Shadows of Consumption: Consequences for the Global Environment*, Cambridge, MA: MIT Press.

Eastwood, L.E. (2011) 'Resisting Dispossession: Indigenous Peoples, the World Bank, and the Contested Terrain of Policy', *New Global Studies*, 5(1): 1–33.

Harvey, D. (2014) *Seventeen Contradictions and the End of Capitalism*, London: Profile Books.

IBON (2012) 'Global Civil Society Workshop on the Rio+20 "Zero Draft" and Rights for Sustainability', unpublished document: agenda and background document for workshop.

Long, S., E. Roberts, and J. Dehm (2010) 'Climate Justice Inside and Outside the UNFCCC: The Example of REDD', *Journal of Australian Political Economy*, 66(summer): 222–46.

McMichael, P. (2012) *Development and Social Change: A Global Perspective*, Los Angeles, CA: Sage.

Pieterse, J.N. (2002) 'Global Inequality: Bringing Politics Back In', *Third World Quarterly*, 23 (6): 1023–46.

Schnaiberg, A. (1980) *The Environment: From Surplus to Scarcity*, Oxford: Oxford University Press.

Takacs, D. (2014) 'Environmental Democracy and Forest Carbon (REDD+)', *Environmental Law*, 44 (1): 71–134.

Verzola, P. Jr. and P. Quintos (2012) *Green Economy: Gain or Pain for the Earth's Poor?* Quezon City: IBON International.

Index

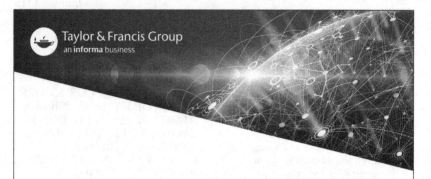

Printed in the United States
by Baker & Taylor Publisher Services